The
GOOD
Divorce

The GOOD Divorce

HOW TO END YOUR MARRIAGE WITHOUT ENDING *YOUR FAMILY*

Karen McNenny

JB JOSSEY-BASS™
A Wiley Brand

CONTENTS

CONTENTS

PROLOGUE

Nobody wants to tell their spouse they are ready to pull the ripcord on their marriage. Certainly not me. I thought having a plan, like packing the parachute before the jump, would help soften the landing, for all of us. My plan for "the talk" included dropping the kids off for a slumber party, so they wouldn't be around for the aftermath. I also packed an overnight bag for myself, afraid my husband might be so angry he'd kick me out on the spot, even though he wasn't that kind of guy. But I knew things would not look the same tomorrow or ever again. The stakes were high. I was scared.

However, on my way back home to have "the talk," I panicked. I wasn't prepared at all. I veered off course and pulled into a bookstore, desperate for guidance on how to break up with the father of my children without destroying our family. I paced up and down the aisles, wrestling with the truth that I was looking for the *Divorce Section*. What I found instead were shelves of battle plans—how to win at divorce, how to get everything you deserve, how to make your ex pay.

I needed to end my marriage, but I didn't want to end my family. I cherished our love story and the beautiful children we made together, but clearly the marriage chapter was coming to a close. I was paralyzed by the idea of divorce, and the mere thought of it was keeping me stuck in a rapidly eroding marriage.

Ten years later, that desperate night at the bookstore led me to my life's work. What started as my personal journey to have a "good divorce" evolved into a mission to transform how America approaches divorce. As a mediator, co-parenting specialist, and divorce consultant working directly with families, I've seen firsthand how the divorce industrial complex—from predatory lawyers to punitive banking practices to outdated workplace policies—exploits families at their most vulnerable. A system designed to support families has instead become an industry that profits from their pain.

This book traces my path from that panicked night at the bookstore, through my own divorce journey and eventually becoming an advocate for family-centered divorce reform. It's a story about redefining success in relationships, about finding peace in completion rather than failure, and about having the courage to challenge a system that focuses on profits over families.

However, this isn't just a critique of a broken system. It's a love story about family—my family—one that doesn't end with divorce but evolves into something new. It's about finding a middle path between staying in my unhappy marriage and destroying my family through divorce. It's about how a galvanizing moment with my kids, and a plate of nachos, affirmed I was on the path to a happier, better version of myself. It's about the conversations I have with my young adult children now, which have shown me we didn't fail at all—in fact, we've succeeded at building something different, but equally beautiful.

As both someone who has lived this journey and who now guides others through it, I've seen how desperately we need to change the divorce narrative. Beyond my personal story, this book is a call to action—to reform the policies and practices that keep families trapped in destructive patterns, to challenge the assumption that divorce will be devastating, and to create a new framework for how we handle relationship transitions in America.

There has been so much emphasis placed on the legal act of getting divorced, yet little attention has been given to divorce education. As a society, we are neglectful of families going through divorce. We should, and can, do better. Parents need access to education and support. So, within these pages, I will share my impetus and design for the Good Divorce Academy. Throughout the book you will find The Good Guide, which includes insights, strategies, and tools that can help usher in a good divorce experience. To be clear, I am pro-family and pro-marriage, and I desperately wish my family had been able to stay in one home, but it didn't go that way for us. And it doesn't go that way for a lot of couples (which is a problem for another day). As long as there are divorces happening, we need to get better at them.

I will begin each chapter with a personal reflection about my experience from the early days of my divorce journey, reminding you that you are not alone. Between chapters, you will find an episode excerpt from my podcast *The Good Divorce Show*. These selections are intended to illustrate what a good divorce can look and sound like. I encourage you to follow the QR code provided to listen to the entire episode. May these personal stories inspire you and provide hope as you navigate your own journey.

My story proves that divorce doesn't have to destroy families. Sometimes, when we have the courage to end what isn't working, we create space for something better to emerge. While society still views divorce as a tragedy, I've discovered it can be a tool for transformation, not just for individual families, but for how we think about love, commitment, and the many ways we can be family.

AUTHOR'S NOTE

These events are presented as I remember them. To protect the privacy of those involved, all names have been changed; any resemblance to actual people or events is purely coincidental. The dialogue throughout this book is not intended as a verbatim transcription but as a creative reconstruction drawn from my recollection of conversations and experiences. Exception is given to *In Their Own Words*, which uses real names and verbatim transcripts from conversations I had with guests on *The Good Divorce Show*.

CHAPTER ONE

THE LOVE

REFLECTION: POORLY MARRIED

The waiting room at our therapist's office was weirdly familiar. Eight years earlier, David and I held our wedding rehearsal dinner in the identical building next door. Built in the early 1900s at Fort Missoula, Officers Row is a beautiful centerpiece of large, white, two-story homes with grand front porches, all circling the open grassy commons. The place where we started our marriage would now become the place we would end our marriage.

I held my breath as I pushed open the building's oversized solid wood door, dreading what was yet to come. The low September sun cut through the tall double-pane windows, illuminating the dust in the air, dancing its way through the waiting room. The soft rounded divots in the parquet floor reminded me that I wasn't the first wounded person to walk down this hallway. I exhaled.

David was already seated in a chair in the waiting room. Of course he was early—he's always early. I'm always running late, making everyone around me absolutely crazy, stressed, and irritated. We've known each other for more than two decades—the same habits still persist; this is who we are.

When our therapist ushered us in, I settled on the right side of the small grey sofa as David took the wingback chair to my right. We were side by side, but not together. Esther seated herself in her usual rocking chair, which appeared to have been pulled right out of a hobbit's house. An intricate weave of willow branches created a throne of wisdom in which she sat. Her wisp of gray hair was always swept up into a perfectly symmetrical bun, which sat perfectly on top of her head.

She had a Mary Poppins mystique around town. She seems like a nice old lady who sits in a rocking chair and nods her head. But watch out, she is going to shake you up—and do it with a teaspoon of sugar. You won't know what hit you. *Yes, that's pretty much what happened. She was finally the therapist who wouldn't just ask us,* "How do you feel about that?" *She really challenged us to take a good look at our marriage and get to some hard truths. She didn't let us get away with* truthiness.

"So," she began, her voice steady and kind as we settled into our seventh month with her, "did you both have a chance to complete the worksheet assignment from last session?"

We both nodded.

"Great," she said. "Who would like to start?"

I looked over at David, but he just stared straight ahead at Esther.

"Um, I'll go first," I began. "I've been working through a lot of this past trauma stuff with my own therapist for a couple of decades. I think I can approach it with an open mind and open heart."

Esther nodded. I spoke aloud, reviewing my worksheet, sharing personal observations and past stories about my unhealthy patterns and how they tie into my trauma experiences and triggers. I felt safe in the space we created and was pining for a shared breakthrough, a moment of new discovery, a thread that could sew us back together.

"David?" Esther prompted. "What did you discover as you did the assignment?"

David shifted his position, crossing his arms. "I don't feel comfortable discussing it here."

My eyebrows lifted and my face most certainly had the are-you-kidding-me expression.

His jaw hardened and he began to spin his wedding ring, a telltale sign that something difficult was about to go down. "I don't need you to tell me about me," he snapped. "And I certainly don't need to lay it all out here. I don't feel safe doing any of this with her in the room," gesturing my way. It's always interesting when one person starts to refer to the other person as if they aren't present in the conversation, as if they don't deserve to be spoken to directly.

"Not with me in the room?" I asked, "Isn't that the point?"

"We all know where this is headed," he said firmly. I could figuratively see the dead end. *"This isn't helpful. None of this is helpful." And he began to stuff his assignment back into his shoulder bag as he prepared to leave.*

Esther quietly watched our exchange, rocking slowly, hands held in her lap. She didn't jump in to referee; she simply let us duke it out for a bit until we both fell silent.

"Well, how would you like to proceed?" she said simply. Which is just about the dirtiest trick in the therapist playbook.

"What do you mean?" I asked, panic rising in my chest.

At our very first couples' session, she asked us a very direct question: "Why are we here, and when will we know we are done?"

I honestly don't remember what David's response was seven months ago, or if he even had one. I suspect I jumped in first, "We are here to decide if we are staying married or getting divorced. We will be done when we know the answer to that question. Either way, we'll have a forever relationship, so we need to protect the future of our family."

A few months into our time with Esther, she made a stark observation about us: "It seems the two of you are poorly married," her words carried no judgment, just a clinical observation. I had never heard that phrase before, poorly married, but it immediately rang true. In some weird way, it felt like a diagnosis. "Yes that's it, we have Poorly Married Syndrome. There is a cure, it's called divorce." It was as if she'd handed us a permission slip to be more logical and less emotional about the whole situation. This wasn't about good people or bad people, this was about are we good or bad together?

It felt as if all the air had been sucked out of the room. David turned his head and stared out the window. I looked at Esther, waiting for her to say more, to offer some final piece of wisdom or hope. But she simply sat there … rocking, calm, present.

"So, that's it?" I finally asked. "We're … done?"

"That's for you to decide," she replied. "But I can't help you further if you don't feel safe enough to engage in the process. I think my work here is done."

She actually said it: "My work here is done." And I don't resent her for it. I think it's a wise decision for therapists to break up with clients that cannot, or will not, make progress. It's an ethical decision and kind to be clear with the couple—to release them. She stated her work was done, but now what were we going to do about it?

David said nothing as we walked out, down the creaking wooden steps of the building's stately porch and into the parking lot. He walked to his car, as I walked to mine. Silence. I put my hand on the steering wheel and was blinded by the pain of looking at my wedding ring. I removed it, placed it in the little coin holder between the car's front seats, and burst into tears.

A NEW NARRATIVE

Divorce is not a weapon; it is a tool. A tool for transformation. A tool to help reconstruct a family that lives in one home, into a family that lives in two homes. Still they're a family, forever.

As I faced the looming truth that my marriage was coming to an end, the last thing I wanted was to become another statistic in America's $13.1 billion divorce industry, where legal professionals profit from conflict and families are treated as collateral damage.[1] Yet everywhere I looked, the message was clear: I was doomed to either stay miserable in my marriage or traumatize my family through divorce.

Why take a bad marriage, spending thousands of dollars, and sometimes years, battling it out in court only to make it all worse? It's senseless. If you simply want it to worsen, stay in your bad marriage. If you want it to get really bad, hire a couple of lawyers who are financially incentivized by ongoing conflict, and let them hijack your family and drain your kids' college funds. Not to mention the long-term damage and trauma that is left in the wake of parents who once shared a love story and still have to find a peaceful way to co-parent. What a terrible idea!

The popular narrative tells us divorce equals failure—that it negates the love that was shared and destroys the family unit forever. But what if we're looking at it all wrong? What if ending a relationship doesn't have to mean ending the family? What if divorce, handled thoughtfully, could improve family dynamics? Isn't that the point of divorce, to make things better?

---

[1] Diment, Dmitry. (2025). Family Law & Divorce Lawyers in the US—market research report (2015–2030). Ibisworld (June). https://www.ibisworld.com/united-states/industry/family-law-divorce-lawyers/4814/?utm_source (Accessed November 24, 2025).

LOOKING FOR A SIGN

At home, my marriage had me tied up in knots of confusion and conflict. We were stuck. I was stuck. There was so much I loved about our family and the life we created, but David and I had numerous incompatibilities, which created constant conflict in our home. I wrestled with what to do, my mental health suffered, and my grace as a parent was evaporating. Desperate for clarity, I asked the universe for a sign—any sign—telling me to stay or go.

Did I really want to blow up my family's life, rupture the very foundation of the commitment we'd built over the years, just for what? A temporary escape from my deep unhappiness? The possibility of meeting someone better? A life filled with greater ease and joy?

I couldn't see past the options in front of me: a contentious and frustrating marriage, or a divorce pitting my husband and me against each other with our beloved children caught in the middle. I didn't want to be destroyed by my creeping depression, but I wasn't sure I could live with myself if I broke up our family.

My husband was a kind man and a good father. We made a good parental team. Maybe our struggles were normal married struggles, and they would get better with time when the kids were older and required less from us. *Just give it time*, I told myself.

TO HAVE AND TO HOLD

I love Love. Most people do. Many watch rom-coms, download dating apps, and, when they find a partner, they relish the experience of being part of a couple and the wonder that is their partner. And why wouldn't they? Love is lovely.

Despite my desire for love, I had all but given up on finding "the one" before I met my husband. At 31, I was O-V-E-R the dating scene: the disappointing options, my own bad choices, the single life, and the invisible label deeming me "too old" for the dating market. I wanted consistency. I wanted love. I wanted a family.

There were partners throughout my twenties, but none of them were quite right, and many were unhealthy relationships. I had finally found a great therapist to help me reflect and work through some bad habits of my dating life. However, the right partner for me was still elusive at best.

So, I settled into the single-woman storyline instead. I had a decent job and some career momentum. I bought my first house, a tiny 1940s home in my hometown. When my name appeared in the phone book next to my new landline number, I was so thrilled that I ripped out the page and hung it on my fridge. My name, in the phone book! Surely, this was proof that I was finally a grown-up. Deep down, however, I wanted that holy grail of secure adult love: I wanted a marriage partner.

Per our Wednesday ritual, I sat in the window seat at our usual bistro with my usual group of girlfriends. It was a crisp bluebird day in October. Out of nowhere, Rhonda began needling me about my solo relationship status.

"McNenny, why are you still single?" Rhonda asked, playfully accusatory, as if I was boycotting the possibility of being swept off my feet. "I know someone who's interested in you."

"Oh really?" I replied, trying to play it cool. "Tell me more."

"Well, he's a musician …" she said, quickly adding, "but he's got a real job, with health benefits!"

"Well, that's a good start," I laughed.

"He's a nice guy," she continued, "emotionally mature, talented, active, respected in the community." She punctuated this statement by spearing a few lettuce leaves. "And you already know each other," she added with a wink.

"Huh," I mused. "Doesn't sound like anyone I know. If I did, I'd probably be dating him already." I took a sip of my drink, careful not to get my hopes up in front of my friends and dreading the possibility of another heartbreak.

"His name is David," she said. She offered up his last name too, and I immediately got butterflies. "He remembers you too, and was wondering if you were single."

I did know this musician with a real job. It had been a few summers since I had interacted with him, which I remembered being pleasant enough. But there were no sparks of romance then, and I was dating someone else at the time. Now, there was a plot twist: we were both single at the same time. I was so flattered that he remembered me. He was a man-about-town and a great catch.

"So, can I give him your number?" Rhonda asked, already tapping away on her phone.

"I don't think you need to go that far. If we're supposed to meet and connect, fate will bring us together."

"Fate, shmate! I think you would make a great couple, and I should give him your number." Rhonda proclaimed.

"Whatever you say," I waved a hand at her comment. "We both know you're going to do whatever you want anyway." And she did.

Before I'd emptied the last moving box into my new home, my phone rang. I shimmied my way through misplaced furniture and located my landline phone tucked in the corner of the living room behind an over-flowing laundry basket and a plant that needed hospice care. I grabbed the phone's yellow handle and tried to untwist its cord as I answered.

"Hello?"

"Oh, hi Karen, it's David. Rhonda gave me your number."

Over the course of a couple of weeks, we shared late night phone calls that continued long past our bedtime. He was easy to talk to, interesting, and interested in me. It quickly became clear we were both smitten and wanted to meet up. I didn't want to commit to an actual date, however, those stakes seemed too high for my tender heart. I was so scared of getting my hopes up and having them dashed, again. So, I invited him to join me at a casual dance performance at the university.

"That sounds great. When shall I pick you up?" David enquired.

"I will be coming from a work gig out of town, so I will just meet you there." This was the perfect solution to my preferred transportation strategy—separate—in case I needed to make a swift escape after the show.

We met in the window-filled lobby of the theater. He was taller than I had remembered at 6'2". We weren't strangers, but we weren't friends, either. Friendly, yes. After negotiating the odd moment of indecision—do we wave, shake hands, hug (we hugged, not too awkward)—we made our way into the performance space. As the concert progressed, he sidled up closer to me until our biceps gently made contact, sending a welcome warmth and excitement through my body.

Stay cool Karen. Remember what your therapist said, go slow. Don't jump into intimacy. Build a friendship. Do your homework. Get to know each other. Don't write the story before you know the story. Don't project your every wish and dream onto this poor innocent bystander. Definitely too soon to start thinking about baby names.

That subtle connection between our biceps also transmitted a message to the side of our knees, which relaxed just enough to lean into a suspended dance of support as we sat closer and closer to each other. It was nice. After the concert, David invited me out for a nightcap. We agreed to go sit by the fire at the cozy lounge down the street.

"Great, I'll meet you there," I said, holding my boundary of independence.

"We can go together. I have room in my car," he persisted. No one wants to feel rejected on the first date, especially me. In solidarity, I relinquished my staunch independence for a hot minute and let him wiggle his way into my heart, as I wiggled into the front seat of his car.

We sat across from each other at a table for two, close to the fire, excited to be connecting, laughing, and telling stories. Basically, getting swept off our feet. It felt easy and exciting. All the love drugs started to work their blinding biological magic.

After a couple of hours of rich and interesting conversation, we started to gather our coats. In one long breath of courage I blurted out, "I really like you, and I want you to know I have the urge to kiss you, but I am not going to kiss you goodnight because my therapist advised that I take things slow; and I wanted you to know, so you don't feel rejected because I do like you and I would like to see you again."

"Ha, that's very thoughtful. I would like to kiss you, too, Karen. But no rush. I totally respect that boundary and I am a patient man." Damn, he's such a heart-wiggler.

The next morning, I awoke with a glow of hope, comforted by the lace of fall frost knitting together a world that felt so frayed just 24 hours ago. The yellow phone rings, jolting me and the hospice plant back into the moment.

"Good morning." His voice is rich with round tones, and it comforts me. "How did you sleep?"

"Oh hi. Sleep was a little distracted. But in a good way." Cheeks stretched across my face in full smile mode, still a little fatigued from all the smiling I had done the night before.

"Yeah, me too. It was nice to reconnect and catch up. Hey, I don't want to slow down your day; I know you have a lot of unpacking you need to do. I just wanted to say thanks for a really great night and that I left a little something outside your front door. Hope you don't mind; I couldn't help myself."

As I opened the front door, a small paper bag tipped over onto the threshold and rested on my big toe. I knew, even before I picked it up, what he had been doing after we said goodnight. As I grabbed the bag, the thin square shape left no question in my mind: I had just received a mix tape (well the modern version, a CD). But the concept and commitment of a curated mix of music, chosen especially for one person, stands the test of time and change in technology. This was a big deal and a pure expression of his love.

A MIX TAPE
A Mix for Karen from David 11/24/02:

1. Let Us Go Laughing—Bruce Cockburn
2. Just Keep Me Moving—k.d. Lang
3. Big Sky Country—Chris Whitley
4. These Days in an Open Book—Nancy Griffith
5. Diggin Me—Martin Sexton
6. Good Thing—Patty Larkin
7. Urge For Going—Joni Mitchell
8. Reasons Why—Nickel Creek
9. Transcendent Blues—Steve Earle
10. Every Little Thing (He) Does Is Magic—Shawn Colvin
11. Follow Through—David Hedges
12. Drawn to the River—Sarah McLachlan
13. Stay—Alison Krauss
14. The Trumpet Vine—Kate Wolf
15. Light House—James Taylor
16. Morning Side—John Gorka

We continued our courtship with long walks and indulged in even longer conversations. We enjoyed the pulsating social scene that is born into a mountain town with too many extroverts living in the same valley. We strolled through First Friday Gallery Nights, rubbing elbows with the local who's who and making a "soft announcement" about our budding romance. Admittedly, we both enjoyed seeing everyone, and being seen by everyone.

> *Oh, now tell me, how did you two meet?*
> *I didn't realize you knew each other.*
> *Oh wow—it's about time you two met.*
> *This totally makes sense, the two of you.*

All the things two smitten, middle-aged, slightly eager, totally romanced, hijacked adults want to hear from their community. *Yes, go forth and procreate. You have the perceived approval and support of your community* (which evidently mattered to us). In a series of grown-up slumber parties, we began to enjoy my little home together. We didn't spend any time at his apartment, which gave me pause. But he was also in the middle of a move, so I dismissed my uneasiness as circumstantial.

When I finally had the courage to bring up the subject, I was met with levity. "If you came to my apartment right now, you would probably stop dating me." We both laughed it off, and I continued to see only what I wanted to see.

We carried on with the intoxicating experience of falling in love. Here was a handsome, artistic, loving man who also wanted the same joy-filled marriage I did, complete with children. We aligned with the future goals that mattered—marriage, kids, community—and we both had steady work to support those goals. He was nine years older than me, never married, and just as eager to exit the dating market as I was. The surge of oxytocin in my brain was matched only by the dancing eggs in my ovaries. We were both so enamored with each other, the only logical next step, after dating for five months, was to get engaged.

We were married four months later, in the same location as our first date—the theater.

We created a meaningful and beautiful wedding day for ourselves and our community. Our guests might have paused to wonder, "Are we going to a musical production or a wedding ceremony?" There was a set designer, a lighting designer, and a musical director. The ceremony included a West African drum procession, jazz trio, string quartet, 16-voice choir, 18-piece big band, and an accordion.

After the ceremony was complete, the guests followed the West African drum procession out of the theater, through the lobby, and out onto the theater's main veranda where a vintage BMW R90/6 was sitting. One of

David's treasures. We bounded out of the atrium doors into a love bath of friends and family. After our getaway on the motorcycle, we met all of our guests downtown in the ballroom of the historic Florence Hotel, complete with a big band to dance the night away. Our matchmaker, Rhonda, sang *At Last*, made famous by Etta James, for our first dance.

LOFTY EXPECTATIONS

I had married the man of my dreams, nine months after our first blind date; it might have been my first mistake. Additionally, it has nothing to do with who David is or isn't. It's the trap we all fall into, when we place our expectations on others. It often leads to disappointment and resentment. How can I ever be angry with David for being exactly who he is? It isn't a question of good vs. bad. It's a question of compatibility.

Dreams aren't based in reality, and it's hard to get a grasp on reality in just nine months. In retrospect, I feel like I had bought the "house" without doing the home inspection: *the curb appeal is so charming, good bones, lots of potential. Who doesn't love a fixer-upper?* We appeared to be a compatible couple, even to ourselves, but not in the ways that would matter long term.

We took a month-long honeymoon through Tahiti, New Zealand, and Mexico, and returned home to start a family. Anya was born 16 months after our wedding day. With the arrival of our daughter, we fell in love all over again: with each other and with the beautiful, tiny human we had created together. It was glorious. Eighteen months later, our son Dwyer was born—another perfect little addition to our perfect little family. We went from a blind date to family of four in 2.5 years. However, it didn't take long before we began to experience the dissonance between our public-facing selves as a couple about town, and our private life as co-parents, lovers, and roommates. They were not in the same world.

The voice of my therapist quietly echoed in the distance: *Go slow, Karen. Don't start with intimacy. Build a friendship. Do your homework. Get to know each other.*

When I was pregnant with Anya, David and I started cycling through marriage counselors. The incompatibilities that I had chosen to ignore or not fully examine during our courtship, were now coming into full view. Our fraught conversations around money, taxes, the state of the garage, how to spend our free time, household chores, and date night (with or without sex), simply could not be ignored any longer.

And for the love of God, why can't that man sensibly and strategically load a dishwasher, so there are no dishes left in the sink to face in the morning! Why, I ask you? When I snapped, I became a dishwasher rearranger, and I knew we were in trouble. Reloading someone else's dishwasher is the first, subtle, sneaky sign of contempt.

According to the Gottman Institute, a researched-based organization dedicated to discovering what makes couples succeed or fail, contempt is the #1 predictor of divorce. Contempt carries with it a poison that seeps into personal interactions. It can take many forms, including hostile humor and sarcasm, mockery, name-calling, and mimicking. Dr. Gottman says, "Contempt is sulfuric acid for love. It is the most poisonous of all relationship killers."[2]

We'd start sessions with one therapist, stick with them for a while, and then stop, only to restart six months later with different therapists. Rinse and repeat. We did this numerous times, with three different therapists, over the course of our short-lived marriage.

The further along we went in our counseling cycle, the more concerned I became. It seemed David and I would always need help with our marriage. Being together simply took an increased effort from both of us to keep the marriage humming harmoniously. Shouldn't there be some intrinsic ease with a partner that you love deeply?

---

[2] Lisitsa, Ellie. (2014). The trouble with contempt. The Gottman Institute (March 5, 2014). Updated March 4, 2024. https://www.gottman.com/blog/the-trouble-with-contempt/.

What was the alternative? I would mull over questions like, *What if we separated? Could I support myself? Where would we all live? Would we doom our kids to a childhood full of trauma? Would lawyers destroy any remaining dignity we had?* I was deeply discouraged by the state of our marriage, but I feared the repercussions of divorce more.

We both read numerous books on how to save a marriage, including *The Seven Principles for Making Marriage Work* by John Gottman, *Boundaries in Marriage* by Henry Cloud and John Townsend, *How to Save Your Marriage* by Sarah Mitchell, to name a few. We really took to heart the effort of saving our marriage. That's what couples do; they fight for their marriage. And yet, deep down, I think we were both looking for some kind of off-ramp. But neither of us would admit it, so we both kept putting in the effort, heading down a one-way road leading to divorce.

In our case, our marriage wasn't always horrible. That's the torment of a good-enough marriage, and the reason why so many of us stay too long; it's just not black and white.

BEND IN THE ROAD

As we approached our eighth wedding anniversary, I was scheduled to speak at a conference in Bend, Oregon. Since it was July, David and I decided to add a family vacation onto my work trip. (Because nothing says "fun" quite like being in a failing marriage and being trapped in a minivan for eight days with two kids under the age of six.) We stuffed the van with camping gear, and more snacks than any human should be allowed to eat on one road trip, and headed for the Oregon Coast.

Our first stop was the Perkins Restaurant off I-90 in Coeur d'Alene, Idaho. As I slid open the minivan's side door, a pool noodle and bag of Cheez-Its tumbled out.

"Get your shoes on, kids. We all have to wear shoes in the restaurant."

"I don't have shoes," Anya declared.

"Yes, I know, that's why I want you to find them and get them on your feet, so we can get into the restaurant, so that we can order food, so we can eat and can get back on the road before it gets dark," answered my impatient, irritated, and hangry voice.

"Mama, I don't have shoes *here*."

I paused and considered her response, hollering across the van to David.

"David, did you put shoes in the car for Anya? Was she wearing shoes when she got in the van?"

"No, and, I don't know," came his response. This time, I let my impatient, irritated, hangry silence convey my message of disappointment and irritation.

So goes the beginning of all family vacations, and the slow erosion of marriages everywhere; an emergency trip to Walgreens must be made to grab all the things you forgot to bring. In this case, we went in search of a new pair of flip-flops and a sense of humor.

The trip could, we hoped, give us a break from our detrimental home-life habits, and instead offer a new perspective on our future. Maybe it would be an opportunity to rekindle the spark we had pre-kids, premarriage. The kids sleeping in the minivan's back seat gave us time to talk and process. We were so deep into our conversation that we missed our exit in central Washington and didn't notice for another hour. Once we realized what we had done, we turned things around. Laughing at ourselves, we wondered if it was a sign that our marriage was equally off course, as we grasped for hope in the mondaine. It was a welcome relief from the standard blame game we were beginning to master.

After the conference in Bend, we did the standard vacationer loop: Crater Lake, Newport Beach, the Oregon Coast Aquarium, and the mighty Redwoods in Northern California. Our first night out we made it to our coastal campsite with plenty of daylight to spare. We took a family walk on the beach before popping up the camper. It was dramatic: rocky cliffs, a roaring sea, dense forest undergrowth, and towering trees. I felt a kind of peace despite the difficult conversations we had on the drive from Bend. The setting seemed fitting: rough, worn, and ever-changing.

We tucked the kids into bed on their side of the pop-up camper before settling in on the opposite side. I scooted closer to David under the blankets, seeking the familiar warmth and comfort of his presence. I pressed up against his back, taking the role of the big spoon. We may have had some tense moments on the drive, but I saw a glimmer of hope too. Maybe this trip really was a chance to start fresh. Maybe we *could* rediscover the connection we'd been missing. Our earlier discussions made me hopeful for our future together. If we were headed toward reconciliation, I couldn't wait to start. I reached out to caress David's arm.

"Hey," I whispered.

David made no move to invite me closer, but I pressed on. I wanted to break through the invisible barrier between us. Just one moment of us coming together could be the catalyst for the bliss-filled marriage we wanted, right? I nestled in closer, resting my head on his shoulder like I had countless times before.

"I miss this," his shoulder supporting my head and my right arm draped across his chest, palm resting on his heart.

I tilted my face up, seeking David's lips for a kiss, craving intimacy and connection. But he turned his head slightly, and my lips grazed his stubbly cheek instead.

"Karen," he sighed, gently pushing me back. "I can't do this right now. It's too hard."

The sting of rejection flooded the corners of my eyes. I felt my stomach drop. I thought we were connecting and making progress. The kids were having a great time. Why couldn't we?

"Okay, I get it," I said. "It's fine." I swallowed the lump in my throat. I gave a sort of pat on his arm and rolled back over to my side. He was right—intimacy was too confusing for both of us right now.

As David's breathing slowed into the rhythm of sleep beside me, I felt wide awake. How were we so far away from one another? I thought this trip—the conversations, the healthy debates—was what we needed. I hungered for clarity—the ambiguity of whether we could mend wounds (and how long it might take) tortured me.

After a few more minutes lying there, I slipped out of bed. I picked up a headlamp and one of the save-your-marriage books I'd brought with us, and I stepped out into the cool night air. Before I turned on the headlamp, I noted the absolute darkness of the night. Clouds hid the moon and stars.

I shuffled over to the still-warm coals of the dwindling campfire, added a few logs, and pulled up my camp chair. Looking at the book in my hands, I made a promise to myself to read it cover to cover—in one sitting. I wanted the secrets to a healed marriage, and dammit, I wanted them *tonight.*

I stayed up until my eyes hurt and my butt went numb. I stayed up until the first rays of morning peeked over the trees. I stayed up until I flipped the very last page. As it turns out, I stayed up for nothing. There was no lightning bolt of clarity, only more questions. No book could tell us if our marriage was worth keeping on life support, or if we should release the marriage and save the family. I snuck back into the camper and climbed into bed, turning away from David.

Back in earshot of David's leveled breathing, I knew three things: I knew I married a good man. I knew I loved the children we created together. And I knew the divide between us was growing daily and becoming intolerable. I certainly didn't see how to end it without leaving a trail of destruction in my wake.

THE PINNACLE OF SUCCESS

Humans are wired for love (or, more dryly, "connection"), and we need connection to survive. From the moment we are born, we seek out the security and comfort of close relationships. As children, we form attachments to caregivers. As we grow, this innate desire for bonding often matures into close friendships and, often, a yearning for intimate, romantic partnerships. People date to find a companion who not only understands and accepts them but also challenges them to grow. The goal of these partnerships, for many, is to build a life together—to weather life's storms and celebrate its triumphs hand-in-hand. It's comforting to share lives with other people, especially loved ones.

Beyond personal comforts, most cultures often tout that it's better to be coupled than uncoupled—to be coupled at all costs. There is no shortage of studies showing that being coupled is better for a person's mental health, social health, and wallets. And although Western culture applauds staunchly independent individuals, the dominant culture still deems long-term romantic partnerships, especially marriage, as the crowning achievement in a person's life. It's unsurprising, then, that most young people (71% in one survey) still think they'll end up marrying.[3]

In all the happy stories I've consumed in my life, couples end up *together*. The epitome of character happiness—the signal to the audience of "happily ever after"—is achieved when a character gets married. Not when they kiss a new partner, not when they move in together, not even when they've successfully navigated "meeting the parents"—the wedding is the marker of the happily ever after, not the marriage that follows.

Even when a person has a great career, a fulfilling social circle, and plenty of therapy under their belts, they still long for a partner. And there are great aspects to having a partner. Life is generally cheaper (shared cost of living), they have a companion to lean on when life gets tough, and often they experience a quality of expansion from exposure to new activities, friends, music, food, and so forth. "Multiply life by the power of two," as one song goes.[4]

---

[3] Brown, Adrianne. (2022). High school seniors' expectations to marry, 2020. Bowling Green State University. https://www.bgsu.edu/ncfmr/resources/data/family-profiles/brown-high-school-seniors-expectation-to-marry-2020-fp-22-04.html.

[4] Indigo Girls (1994). Power of Two. Track 5 on *Swamp Ophelia*. Epic, CD.

Marriage feels like the pinnacle of success for any couple. It signals to others "she has made it" or "he has settled down." There is a finality to marriage ("until death do us part"), and a safety in being more firmly tied to one another. There's a promise of staying, even when the going gets tough. And, if you choose the right person (fingers crossed), the "tough going" will be more manageable together.

I believed in the common knowledge surrounding relationships and marriage. I had few reasons to doubt it. When David and I got married, I thought I knew all I needed to know. I'd seen my parents' marriage and learned from it, mostly what I didn't want in a marriage. I'd seen friends' marriages and asked them for their keys to success. I read books on how to be in a successful relationship. I went to therapy—for years—on my own to be a better partner. All of it taught me to believe the love David and I shared meant we could make it through anything together.

HOLD THE MAYO

Intimate relationships are more complicated than most people admit. All the romantic movies, books, TV shows, and articles online don't show the ugly parts of relationships, unless the struggles make the ending more satisfying. But anyone who's been in a relationship knows the hard parts don't always lead to richer, deeper connections. When those complicated moments rear their heads in a relationship, many don't know how to handle them. There is no standard course in school for interpersonal communication, let alone communication with an intimate partner. And while there are plenty of resources on saving a relationship, how to be a better partner, and recovering from a bad relationship, there aren't many guides for how to make an elegant exit.

I was recently asked about the common mistake of staying too long in a dying marriage, which can lead to irreversible damage to the family unit and co-parent relationship. A marriage can often be like a jar of mayo with little flecks of mold growing at the edges. You look in the jar, scoop off the sprouts of fungus, and put it back in the fridge. To the naked eye, most of that jar is still good mayo. You can ignore the mold for a little bit, but it inevitably grows back. What's left in the jar has already started to go bad—it's tainted. But you can't just throw away the entire jar, can you?

Mayo aside, divorce typically looks like a terrible option. According to common wisdom, leaving a partnership can be even worse than sticking it out and will certainly scar your children for life. Extended families split down battle lines. Friends try to understand both partners but often end up choosing sides. Acquaintances rubberneck and try to unearth every little detail of why it ended and whose fault it was. The love story, which once looked so promising, has a tragic ending. Marriage is exalted as the pinnacle of relationship success. And if marriage is the ultimate success, then divorce is the ultimate failure.

I didn't want to fail. I couldn't bear to have the father of my children become my enemy, as we faced off in a divorce over the kids and our belongings. Divorce meant legal fees—big ones—and drawing battle lines. Divorce meant yelling at each other across conference tables with lawyers watching. It also meant having to tell our children. And the one that gutted me the most, it meant forfeiting 50% of my bedtime snuggles and morning dance parties with my kids. Half! How could I possibly relinquish half of their childhood in the name of divorce? I couldn't begin to imagine this reality.

NO GOOD OPTION

All the books I could find on divorce pitched a heartbreaking, family-severing narrative that I couldn't—wouldn't—participate in. My options seemed to be, stay and grow increasingly miserable, or leave and blow up my life. Either way, I was going to feel awful! I was doomed to live unhappy in a marriage or leave and cause unhappiness for others. This loop kept me in my marriage, and it's why I fought so hard to save it.

However, the misguided societal advice and expectations about marriage and divorce—or, more broadly, relationships and breakups—keep couples together well past their expiration date. People who can't reconcile stay together in loveless marriages. Some couples take out their misery on others—their kids, their family members, employees, and friends. Some take it out on themselves, devolving into a lackluster or angry version of themselves. Some transition to being no more than roommates, leading separate lives while living in the same home.

Some begin to seek imposed reasons to end the relationship (e.g. affairs, betrayal, abuse, and addiction)—a rupture that can justify the end of the relationship to the imaginary judge and jury in our heads. Yet, thinking there is no alternative to staying in a bad marriage or going through a destructive divorce is a toxic binary, and it ruins lives.

On the darkest of days, I began to see death as a better ending than divorce. I saw it as less complicated, less expensive, and less drawn out. If just one of us could stumble into some fiery tragedy, the marital suffering would end. Truly, who thinks like this? As it turns out, it's more common than I thought. As a divorce consultant, over the years, I have heard many variations of this dark prayer. How is it that the divorce machine has become so broken, that people would rather die than walk through the hot coals of the court system?

Short of a fatal accident, my other option was to take things into my own hands. I imagined the location: an especially tight and curvy section of Highway 200, at the top of Rogers Pass. I would simply swerve on the ice, hoping the minivan would topple over the guardrail, killing me instantly and painlessly, as I plummeted into the deep valley in a fiery implosion. At least this way, there would be insurance money for David and the kids to claim, if it was deemed an accident. I felt confident I could make it look like one.

That fantasy stayed with me for longer than I'm comfortable admitting. It spun around in my head as a viable exit strategy. It wasn't that my marriage was abusive or destructive. Divorce was what I feared, not my husband. In the moment, death looked like a better option than the typical divorce outcome of becoming enemies with the father of my children. I was horrified by my thoughts, but also desperate to avoid the inevitable destruction of divorce.

However, as I walked with my longtime friend, Cynthia, on a warm summer night, I found my turning point.

As I lamented about the hardships at home, Cynthia stopped, looked at me intently, and asked, "Hey, are you thinking about a plan?"

"What?" I replied. "No, I don't have a plan. That's the problem. I don't know what to do. I don't know how to stay, and I don't know how to leave. I am living in a prison of indecision and paralysis. It is a daily torment!"

Cynthia looked me in the eye and clarified, "No, not *that* kind of plan."

The realization hit me. Fiery explosions, icy roads, an accident. I *did* have a plan. I felt the color drain from my face.

"You need to call your therapist first thing tomorrow," she replied. It felt like a warning.

I was in relationship purgatory, but I wasn't stuck between a good place or a bad place—both options in front of me looked terrible. Had I known of a middle path (one with less destruction, despair, and debt), I might've decided sooner. I might've been able to exit without doing more harm. But as it was, I had stayed too long, and we all suffered the consequences. In the absence of a clearly marked exit, I acted like a kamikaze pilot with no other option but to dive bomb, ensuring a fiery ending.

After too many months of dark thoughts, what I really needed was a new option. I wanted a way out that didn't involve destroying my life, or the lives of my children or David. I didn't want to choose between a bad marriage or a worse divorce. That is no choice at all.

CHAPTER TWO

THE SYSTEM

REFLECTION: THE CLASSROOM OF DIVORCE

Lawyers may get us divorced, but who is going to teach us how to be divorced?

I walked into the basement of a nondescript 1960s era office building on the Clark Fork River. Ten weary parents squished into a bland basement room, with no view. The videos being shown were outdated role-plays of hostile parent situations, complete with bad acting and misguided advice.

David and I had just begun the divorce process, and we were looking for guidance. When we called the local family resource center to register for a co-parent class, we were told we couldn't attend together. That should've been our first clue.

The plastic chairs around me were filled with heavy-hearted, beaten-down parents who couldn't have possibly attended this class with their ex. It quickly became apparent all of these parents were in high conflict divorces. Some had been court ordered to attend. I sat in terror, hearing their stories. I was looking at the ruins of a broken system.

They were dumbfounded to hear about my relatively peaceful experience. Having a low-conflict divorce shouldn't be a thing of wonder and surprise, it should be the norm.

One woman shared how her ex hid their shared assets. A man described his ex-wife "poisoning" their children against him. Another recounted a battle that took place in the Walmart parking lot, while the kids transitioned between cars. Story after story reinforced the narrative that divorce meant war, ex-spouses were enemies, there will be a winner and a loser, and the best you can hope for is a well-fortified truce.

This wasn't a class for people like David and me, who were just trying to get unmarried. We wanted to restructure our family, thoughtfully. This was crisis management for high-conflict divorces. We were literally and figuratively in the wrong class, but there was no other option offered.

The instructor, a mental health specialist teaching an archaic curriculum, was describing the different kinds of relationships that might develop post-divorce: Adversarial, Distant, Businesslike. The last category he wrote on the board said Friends. I exhaled and released my fear just enough to allow hope to make an appearance.

"Friendship," the instructor punctuated, "is the most dangerous relationship you can have with your ex."

If I had been drinking a glass of water, it would have been a classic spit take. Did I hear that right? I challenged him, "Why would you say that? What could possibly be dangerous about parents developing a friendship postdivorce?"

He carried on with jargon and went on to describe scenarios of manipulation, of exes taking advantage of each other, and children being used as pawns. Every example assumed conflict, deceit, and hostility between former spouses. I went dead inside.

I didn't expect us to be besties, but did we have to be enemies? I realized friendship was a lofty goal, but I was just hoping we could be friendly. Most people would agree that David and I are naturally friendly people. Why should that be any different under these circumstances?

We survived our extracurricular co-parent course and moved on with the court-sanctioned educational program. Many states require some form of parent/divorce education when children are involved, as a way to strengthen co-parenting skills, encourage positive co-parent communication, and to understand the negative impact parental conflict can have on children. Requirements vary widely across the states. Massachusetts requires around four to five hours.[1] You can get by in Alaska with as little as watching a 19-minute video.[2] In Montana, we were required to attend a two-hour co-parent orientation.

---

[1] mass.gov (2025). Parent education: notice to parents for mandatory co-parenting education course. https://www.mass.gov/guides/parent-education-notice-to-parents-for-mandatory-co-parenting-education-course?utm_source=chatgpt.com (accessed November 24, 2025).

[2] Divorce Parenting Videos (n.d.). Alaska. https://www.divorcevideos.net/alaska.html.

I walked up the worn rotunda marble staircase, in the historical courthouse located in the middle of town, with 50 other sad, bereft, shameful parents. It was a sea of hunched shoulders and hidden faces. None of us wanted to be there, and we certainly didn't want to strike up a conversation with anyone familiar. We stood in line and registered one by one, so the judge would have proof we attended. It was one more checked box in the never-ending administrative decathlon of divorce.

The stunning beauty of the high ceilings, historical murals adorning the walls, and wood-carved benches brought no comfort. I sat at the back of the oversized courtroom, without removing my winter coat or hat, ready to flee. The judge came out of their chamber and sat in the throne of judgment, fully clad in the black robe of power, intimidation, and decision-making. It felt like I was about to be put on trial. It was similar to the irrational wave of anxiety that sweeps over me when I see a police car, even when I'm not breaking the law.

Next up was guidance from a mental health professional, who stood near the judge, separating them from us. A cycle of professionals was basically telling us to behave and not screw up our kids. Their message was well intended, but its delivery felt like punishment and judgment, not the classroom we needed. I began to feel numb, stopped listening, and willed myself not to crumble under the weight of the moment.

My family was ripping apart, along with my heart and identity. We were looking for guidance, support, and education. What we got was a lecture with a side order of shame.

I fled to my car and sank into a cocktail of guilt and devastation.

DIY-ISH

David and I didn't default to the standard of hiring lawyers right out of the gate. We figured we could DIY ourselves through the divorce process. After all, we'd already done the hard parts: we divided our belongings fairly, moved into two houses, agreed on 50/50 time split with the kids, figured out our finances, and built a residential schedule for the kids. We'd collaborated on everything thus far. Surely filling out some paperwork couldn't be that difficult. We'd download the forms, complete them together, and file them with the court. It seemed simple enough.

We did some googling and went to the courthouse's self-help law center. The volunteer on duty that day was entirely underwhelming and not much help. We needed someone to sit down and walk us through the process. Instead, we were shown a bookcase full of documents, as they clarified they weren't able to provide legal advice because we weren't clients. What we didn't realize is that the divorce process had been hijacked by the legal system, creating a situation where most of us become dependent on attorneys to manage the complexities.

We picked up what we thought were the right forms and brought them home to review. As per usual, I took the lead on most of the logistical details, creating spreadsheets for our shared possessions and financial information. There was a bunch of information that David needed to gather from his employer about retirement accounts and health benefits. We found ourselves falling back into old patterns of bickering. The unhealthy dynamic of our marriage now had the potential of poisoning our divorce as well. Which only makes sense, after all, we are the same people.

Our financial separation had been remarkably straightforward. The prenuptial agreement we'd signed years earlier made the larger financial division simple. We preemptively decided whatever assets or debts we brought to the marriage we would leave with. All additional property and assets acquired during the marriage, according to Montana state law, were evenly divided. There wasn't much to discuss beyond that. Compared to the horror stories we'd heard about couples fighting over every piece of furniture and every penny for years, and with great expense in attorney fees, our financial separation appeared to be straightforward.

Generally speaking, people underestimate the business side of getting married and the legal ramifications, should it unravel. I would like to suggest that a prenuptial agreement isn't a negative indication of your love and devotion to each other; it's simply a good business move. I recalled sitting with a corporate attorney as he wrote up the limited liability company (LLC) agreement for a small family-business endeavor I took on with my parents and one of my siblings. I was surprised, when he turned to us early in the process and said, "So, let's talk about what happens when you break up and decide to dissolve the business." Obviously, we would still be family but no longer business partners. That agreement is what protected my family relationships years later, when we predictably dissolved the business. The best time to write a prenup is before you need one.

With all the major decisions behind us, we just needed to make our separation legal. But what seemed straightforward in theory proved maddeningly slow and complicated. We set up a structured schedule to meet every month in a public place (e.g. a coffee shop, a restaurant, the library) to keep us on our best behavior. We'd bring our lists and files, trying to gather essential documents to complete the confusing paperwork. But almost inevitably, these meetings would end in argument. We were great co-parents, but when it came to any serious adulting activity (e.g. dealing with taxes, real estate, money, divorce), we struggled. A pattern became predictable: we'd meet, tensions would rise, someone would walk out, and we'd let things simmer for a few weeks then try again. What should've been straightforward decisions became emotional eruptions. What should've taken months, took years.

After 18 months of starting and stopping, a friend encouraged me to finally hire a lawyer. We had tried DIY, but we weren't making progress and I was tired of it dragging onward. I finally hired a lawyer and encouraged David to do the same.

With lawyers came a new set of frustrations, however. After depositing a sizable retainer and paying hundreds of dollars per hour, my attorney also charged me 0.50/page for photocopies of documents, then charged me again for the time to fix errors they had made (wrong addresses, misspelled names, incorrect birthdates for our children) and then charged me to reprint them again. I wanted to scream, but this was how the system worked. Every phone call, email, and meeting was billable in 10-minute increments—even the minutes when I was sobbing. Those were some expensive tears.

David and I were never in the same room with our attorneys. We became bystanders to our own divorce and future life. The attorneys made phone calls to each other, exchanged emails and documents back and forth at a glacial pace—three weeks to answer a simple question, another three weeks to schedule a meeting.

It would take 27 months from the day we physically separated into two homes, to the day I walked out of the courthouse, finally divorced. Too. Damn. Long. Why had it taken so long? Why wasn't it easier? Why did it feel like the system wanted (and expected) us to be so adversarial? A lot of damage can be done during a drawn-out process, which is why I support families moving through the process as swiftly as possible.

David and I were left to our own devices, which also slowed things down. However, I'm not convinced it would've happened any faster if we'd retained lawyers right away; it would've just cost more. Typically, lawyers aren't financially incentivized to move things along swiftly. Some attorneys will even find new battles to fight, or sabotage mediation so they can go to litigation, where the big bucks are made and families are shredded.

THE EXPLOITATIVE DIVORCE INDUSTRY

During the time of divorce purgatory, I would spend free nights researching divorce. One night I stumbled upon a documentary called *Divorce Corp*. I streamed it immediately, and by the end, I was raging and in tears (again). A fierce advocate started to rise inside of me. I had been living my own difficult story of divorce, now I was seeing the divorce industrial complex for what it was: a money-making machine of destruction.

The film validated everything that I'd come to believe about divorce in America: the system was a predatory industry designed not to help families transition but to extract wealth from them at their most vulnerable moment. "More money flows through the family courts and into the hands of courthouse insiders than in all other court systems in America combined," the documentary stated.[3]

The numbers the documentary presented were staggering and still, in recent years, the industry is robust. The average divorce lawyer charges $270 per hour.[4] Divorce filing fees range from $80 (in North Dakota) to $435 (in California).[5] If you manage to do your divorce on your own, it could cost you less than $1,000. Yet, the average spent on a divorce lawyer is around $11,300 *per spouse*.[6] In high-net-worth or "complex" divorces, the cost becomes even more outrageous. Experienced family law attorneys may bill $500–800 or more per hour, depending on the location. According to CounselPro's guide, fully contested high-asset divorces can result in $50,000–200,000+ per spouse in legal fees.[7]

One scene in *Divorce Corp* had a gray-haired law professor holding up a slim volume of pages between his fingers. "Family law used to be these 30 pages," he said. Next, he picked up a stack of thick volumes, hundreds and hundreds of pages. "Now, this is what family law has become."

The complexity in family law and divorce has expanded, and *Divorce Corp* argues this is intentional. Whether or not it is, the legal system, through financial incentives, encourages adversarial divorces. Every contested issue—homes, retirement funds, pensions, alimony, child support,

---

[3] IMDb (2014). Divorce Corp. Documentary (January 10, 2014). https://www.imdb.com/title/tt2636456/.

[4] Caporal, Jack. (2025). The average cost of a divorce. Motley Fool Money (September 12, 2025). https://www.fool.com/money/research/average-cost-of-divorce/ (accessed November 24, 2025).

[5] Edwards, Sarah. (2023). The most and least expensive states to get a divorce in 2025. Forbes Advisor (November 15, 2023). https://www.forbes.com/advisor/legal/divorce/the-cost-of-divorce-by-state/ (accessed November 24, 2025).

[6] Lawyers.com (2025). The cost and duration of divorce. https://legal-info.lawyers.com/family-law/divorce/cost-duration/ (accessed November 24, 2025).

[7] CounselPro (n.d.). California (CA) High-asset & Complex Divorces. CounselPro. https://www.counselpro.ai/divorce-guide/california/high-asset-complex-divorces?utm_source (accessed November 24, 2025).

and custody—means more billable hours. The longer divorces drag on, the more money lawyers make. There is little incentive for divorce lawyers to move quickly or efficiently.

Near the end of the film, divorcing couples in Scandinavia are interviewed about the divorce process. "Why would we go to court?" one woman asked, genuinely puzzled. "We don't understand why Americans do divorce like that. Here's our child—we'll support our child, we'll support each other." Divorce in countries like Sweden and Norway are handled administratively, instead of through the court system. The process is simple, affordable, and focused on the family's well-being.

I realized then that David and I had been trapped in a system designed for conflict. We'd started with the best intentions to cooperate, but the American divorce industry profits from conflict and drawn-out divorces. One *Divorce Corp* interviewee admitted her divorce took seven years.

What we needed, and what most divorcing couples need, was a guide and a collaborative approach. We needed someone to help us navigate paperwork, understand our options, and make decisions that honored our family's needs. We needed a process of self-determination. Other countries prove that divorce can be handled with dignity, efficiency, and minimal harm done to families. But in America, the $13.1 billion divorce industry has every incentive to maintain the status quo. Every couple who manages to separate amicably represents lost revenue. The system isn't broken; it's working exactly as it was designed, to profit from your pain. What America needs is a new system.

SOCIAL BURDEN

Divorce in the United States is more than a personal upheaval. It's a significant economic event that ripples through families, communities, and society at large. The so-called "divorce industry," encompassing family law attorneys, mediators, counselors, and online service platforms, generates tens of billions of dollars annually. As I've stated before, legal services alone accounted for over $13 billion in projected revenue for 2025, while online divorce platforms and counseling services contribute an additional $4 billion or more. These figures, while staggering, merely scratch the surface. They represent money flowing out of families at the very moment when financial and emotional resources are the most strained, creating a system where vulnerability becomes profitable.

The human cost of divorce extends far beyond market transactions. Household income losses for women, for example, can average 27–30% in the first postdivorce years, translating to roughly $10,000–12,000 per woman per year, while men experience smaller but still significant declines of 10–15% ($3,000–5,000 per year).[8] When multiplied across the roughly 2.5 million divorces per year involving women, these losses alone amount to $25–30 billion annually. Children are not spared either. Long-term studies find that adults whose parents divorced in childhood earn 9–13% less over their lifetimes compared with peers from intact families.[9] Public costs amplify the financial burden. In the United States, divorce is believed to cost taxpayers over $100 billion in social service expenditures annually, including increased welfare, healthcare, housing support, and reduced tax revenue.[10] The economic impact isn't confined to the families themselves but is also distributed across society.

Much of this strain is exacerbated by the incentives embedded in the legal system. Attorneys are often rewarded for conflict, drawn-out proceedings, and complex litigation, rather than cooperation and resolution. This creates an environment where families are encouraged—implicitly or explicitly—to battle, driving up costs and prolonging emotional trauma.

---

[8] PSID/HRS (2020–2025). Panel study of income dynamics/Health and retirement study.

[9] Johnston, A. C., Jones, M. R., and Pope, N. G. (2025). Divorce, family arrangements, and children's adult outcomes. *NBER Working Paper*.

[10] Scafidi, B. (2008). The taxpayer costs of divorce and unwed childbearing. *Institute for American Values* 12, 13.

The system weaponizes moments of vulnerability, turning what could be a cooperative transition into a contest that drains resources, energy, and goodwill. There is a pressing need to simplify the divorce process, reduce costs, and give families permission to separate with dignity, prioritizing cooperation over conflict. Reform isn't only a private concern—it is a public one. Married, divorced, or single, we all have a stake in improving the system, because the economic, social, and intergenerational consequences of divorce ripple through our communities, workplaces, and society as a whole.

DIVORCE TAX

As my husband and I found ourselves battling the legal system, we were also battling the one-household assumptions built into every system we encountered. School registration forms demanded a "primary residence," allotting space on the form for just one address. Emergency contact forms wanted one main number. Medical offices, sports leagues, after-school programs—every single database was designed for families who either lived together under one roof or were locked in conflict with designated "custodial" and "noncustodial" parents. There's no checkbox for functional co-parents with happy kids in two homes.

These systemic limitations were annoying but not damaging. However, the financial hoops of divorce knocked me off my feet. I began to think of it as the "divorce tax"—similar to the "single tax" where unmarried people pay more for everything because they can't split costs with a partner. Now both David and I maintain complete households, each paying housing, utility, and grocery costs on our own.

We split the kids' direct expenses down the middle: summer camps, extracurricular activities, season passes for the local ski hill, piano lessons, and so on. But day-to-day practical items needed to be duplicated to create greater ease for the kids and greater success for us. It usually meant buying two sets of clothes and toiletries, along with books and toys when they were younger. Those duplicate expenses added up quickly, exposing a hidden cost of maintaining stability across two homes.

The first major divorce tax came in January 2012, when the title of our family home would transfer to me. What I thought would be a simple administrative task turned into an expensive lesson in how the mortgage system penalizes divorce.

As I approached the front door of my lender's office, I had to take a deep breath and prepare myself to repeat the narrative again, "Yeah, not what we had hoped for, but not every marriage lasts." Fortunately, my lender was also a divorced mama and understood the struggles firsthand.

"Well, we have decided I will keep the house, per our prenuptial agreement, but David needs to come off the title and mortgage so I can fully assume ownership. What papers do we need to sign?"

She furrowed her brow and took a deep breath, "You aren't going to like this Karen, but that means you have to fully refinance the house."

Now I was furrowing my brow, "What do you mean, as if I was buying my house all over again?"

"Yep, that's what it means."

"But I am the same owner; nothing is really changing," I protested.

"We will have to run all your finances to be sure you qualify for the loan on your own. Then we'll draw up new loan papers that will include an appraisal and closing costs with fees for the title company and filing with the city. Interest rates have gone up, so your monthly payment is likely going to increase as well."

It was insane. I was desperately trying to create some stability for our kids and keep this home, at least for a while. It was important that not everything change for them all at once. We needed to keep our family home. I couldn't hold back the tears, as I pleaded with her.

She slid the Kleenex box in front of me, and said her hands were tied. My original interest rate was considerably lower than the current rates. It translated to a few hundred dollars more each month for the exact same house. I was now solely responsible for the increased monthly payment, plus thousands of dollars in refinancing fees.

How could it be acceptable in this day and age to financially punish families going through divorce? Common sense tells us it's good for kids if adults can keep their world stable and predictable, as much as possible, during divorce. The family home often acts as an anchor for kids, while other parts of their life may feel disorienting. I was ostensibly being pushed out of my home by the mortgage industry.

Loan assumption can be a helpful alternative to refinancing, but many lenders will *not* prequalify a spouse until after the divorce decree is finalized. It creates a difficult bind, as the home is often the largest marital asset, yet key financial decisions in the Marital Settlement Agreement (MSA) require information that lenders refuse to approve until the decree already exists. Without clarity on whether one spouse can actually qualify, couples should include "if-this, then-that" contingencies in the decree, which can avoid future conflict, delays, or a forced sale of the home.

As a divorce consultant, I guide co-parents through the entire scope of their divorce journey; from the day they make the BIG decision, through the completion of the decree. The Good Divorce Method is a process of self-determination. It encourages creativity, collaboration, and early planning, so that couples avoid system-driven pitfalls and preserve the equity in their home, rather than watching conflict drain it away.

THE GOOD GUIDE: HOW TO NAVIGATE THE LOAN ASSUMPTION PROCESS

1. **Gather all financial documents:** including recent pay stubs, W-2s/1099s, tax returns, bank statements, debt schedules, and credit reports.

2. **Request a detailed conversation with your lender early:** ensure you understand their current policies on loan assumptions and divorce-specific requirements.

3. **Obtain a draft or outline of the divorce financial terms (even before the decree):** provide lenders with a clear picture of anticipated support, debts, and asset division.

4. **Secure a copy of the final divorce decree as soon as it is issued:** most lenders will not process assumption applications without it.

5. **Run updated affordability numbers:** confirm your mortgage payments, taxes, insurance, and postdivorce income all align with lender guidelines.

6. **Clarify timelines and contingencies in the MSA:** for example, clarify how long a spouse has to apply for the loan assumption, and what happens if they don't qualify.

7. **Document communication with the lender:** ensure both spouses understand expectations, potential barriers, and next steps.

8. **Act quickly to list, sell, or otherwise transition the home if one spouse cannot qualify:** avoid post-divorce disputes and financial conflict.

DOUBLE TROUBLE

The divorce insurance-penalty revelation came years later when our kids reached driving age. Adding Anya to my car insurance policy triggered an unexpected conversation with my agent. "Both you and David will need to carry both kids on your separate policies," he explained. I argued the logic—they were the same kids, driving the same car between homes, so why should we pay twice? His sympathetic response: "I know it doesn't make sense, but it's how the system works."

The math was staggering. Insurance for two teenage drivers is already expensive, and for us it effectively doubled. Not because they needed more coverage, but because their parents had two addresses. Same kids, same car, twice the price. We were paying double for being responsible divorced parents, who wanted to ensure our children were covered. The principle bothered me more than the money. A single parent would pay once. A married couple would pay once. But two involved, responsible, caring parents who happened to be divorced—we paid twice.

Tax season brought its own special complications. Deciding who would claim the children as dependents created another dilemma and had no clean solution in the IRS framework. Who claims which child, when custody is truly a 50/50 split? We were given two options: one parent claims both kids, or each parent takes one dependent. Once again, we had to fit into the binary box of custodial versus noncustodial parent, there was no box for functional co-parents with happy kids in two homes. Why shouldn't both of us be able to claim all of our children in each household? If anyone should have double-dip tax benefits, it should be single-parent households of divorce.

I recognized our privilege in being able to absorb these financial penalties, although it was a stretch for sure. I could barely afford the double insurance, the duplicate clothes, and the home refinancing fees. We weathered the divorce tax without sacrificing our children's activities or opportunities. But I often think about families who can't shoulder the financial burden and fall into increased conflict because of financial insecurity post-separation.

The systemic bias toward intact families creates real barriers to the kind of collaborative co-parenting that research shows benefits children most. Society hasn't caught up to modern family structures of divorced families, blended families, chosen families, same-sex parents, and multigenerational households. Schools still assume one primary contact. Financial systems assume two-income households. Insurance companies operate as if divorce means one involved parent instead of two. These institutional failures impose real costs on families trying to do right by their children.

The hidden costs of divorce also extend beyond the cost of lawyers and filing the state paperwork. The infrastructure of American life is littered with penalties big and small for choosing a cooperative divorce. We absorbed these costs as the price of the good divorce we were determined to have, but I still rail against the system that makes a good divorce expensive.

NEGLECT

As a society, we are neglectful of divorcing families. Despite being one of the most stressful life events as identified on the Social Readjustment Rating Scale (SRRS), divorce is often overlooked in how we support families during major transitions.[11] The SRRS ranks divorce as the second-highest stressor for adults, surpassed only by the death of a spouse, yet our systems rarely treat it with the same seriousness or structure of care. Families navigating divorce must manage emotional upheaval, shifting identities, legal and financial pressures, and the profound impact on children, all without the coordinated support typically offered for other major life crises.

For instance, the Family and Medical Leave Act (FMLA), enacted in 1993, was designed to protect workers who need time away from their jobs to manage significant family or medical responsibilities, without fear of losing employment. Its primary purpose is to allow eligible employees up to 12 weeks of unpaid, job-protected leave for events such as the birth or adoption of a child, caring for a seriously ill family member, or managing one's own serious health condition.

FMLA represents a major step forward in acknowledging that workers sometimes face unavoidable life circumstances that require both time and

---

[11] Holmes, T. H. and Rahe, R. H. (1967). The social readjustment rating scale. *Journal of Psychosomatic Research* 11, 213–218.

stability to navigate. However, despite covering a range of impactful family events, the law does not include divorce or separation as qualifying situations, even though research shows divorce is one of the most stressful events that any of us will navigate. As a result, employees going through divorce must juggle legal proceedings, emotional turmoil, new parenting logistics, and drastic changes in family structure, without protected time away from work.

Consequently, employees navigating divorce often experience heightened stress, reduced focus, and diminished productivity, which can ripple across the workplace and further compound the personal and professional challenges they face. This lack of recognition leads many parents and children to struggle silently, normalizing distress that deserves intervention. When we ignore the intensity of this stressor, we miss critical opportunities to stabilize families, reduce conflict, and support healthy long-term outcomes.

Looking back, I see how the traditional messaging around divorce, like the high-conflict parenting class, actually perpetuates the very problem we need to solve. By assuming all divorces are high conflict, by teaching defensive strategies rather than collaborative ones, by warning against the "danger" of being too friendly with an ex, these programs and stories create adversarial dynamics where none need to exist. David and I needed resources for thoughtful restructuring, maintaining family cohesion across two homes, redefining our boundaries, and using effective communication strategies. Instead, we got battle training for a war we weren't interested in fighting.

A HOPEFUL ALTERNATIVE

When I established my work as a divorce coach, I was also told that most coaches only support one member of the divorcing couple, which never made sense to me. From the beginning, I set out to work with both parties side by side. I knew the best outcomes would come from parents working together, and I still believe that to be true. The Good Divorce Method is a unique model in the world of divorce but is proving to have wonderful outcomes for families.

However, long before I entered the conversation, other professionals had been hard at work trying to disrupt the industry and offer a better methodology. In 1990, Stuart Webb, a Minneapolis-based attorney, introduced a pioneering alternative known as Collaborative Divorce. Collaborative Divorce emerged when lawyers began to recognize that divorce is primarily a personal relationship issue with legal attachments, and not simply a legal dispute.

Webb, frustrated with the adversarial courtroom process, declared he would no longer litigate divorces. Instead, he would only work with couples willing to negotiate their issues outside the courtroom. If they chose to go to court, he would withdraw and refer them to a more traditional litigator. Other attorneys joined him and formalized the approach: both spouses and lawyers would sign an agreement committing to resolve all issues through good-faith negotiation. If either party opts for court, both lawyers would withdraw. This structure would keep everyone invested in settlement, rather than preparing for a fight.

The model spread across North America, with early adopters reporting dramatic reductions in court involvement. Today, Collaborative Divorce continues to grow and is often less costly than preparing a full litigation case. It remains distinct from mediation: mediation uses one neutral third party, while Collaborative Divorce gives each spouse their own lawyer who provides independent legal advice within a cooperative framework. Other financial, mental health, or child-life professionals are often part of a collaborative team as well.

COLLABORATIVE DIVORCE: PROS AND CONS

Pros:

- Keeps families out of court
- Encourages cooperation and respectful communication
- Is often less costly than litigation
- Allows each spouse to retain their own legal advocate
- Can create more durable, mutually crafted agreements

Cons:

- Can still be expensive, depending on the professionals involved
- Requires full participation from both spouses
- Isn't suitable if there's abuse, coercion, or an extreme power imbalance

IN THEIR OWN WORDS

The Good Divorce Show
Season 1, Episode 2
Jake and Jeni
Married 12 years
No kids, produced seven albums together

Listen to the full episode here:

DIVORCE CELEBRATION

Jake: So, Karen, when we finally made the decision to end our marriage, it felt surreal. After 12 years together, seven albums, multiple national tours, and building a life in music, letting go seemed impossible—but also necessary.

Jeni: It really was. And the part that helped us so much was remembering that love doesn't disappear just because a marriage ends. I still love Jake—I always will—but staying married wasn't healthy for either of us anymore.

Jake: Exactly. And because we both accepted that, the whole process of divorce became collaborative, almost like a project we were tackling together.

Jeni: That's when we had the idea for a divorce party. We knew telling our friends, our students, and our audience over and over again that we were getting divorced would be exhausting. I couldn't have that conversation 200 times, but I could have it once with 200 people.

Jake: It was amazing. We put out an invitation, framed it as a celebration of what we had accomplished together and what was coming next. Over 200 people showed up! Friends, family, bandmates— everyone we cared about. It became the conversation itself: people could see we weren't bitter, we weren't angry. We were moving forward with love.

Jeni: It was goofy too—we ended up wearing practically the same outfit by accident. But the energy was incredible. We hugged, we laughed, and we let everyone witness that this could be done differently. Our bandmates were there. That does set a certain tone. And there was drinking, which was really poor planning on our part, because the next morning we had to be in court at 8:00 a.m. and for a musician that's an ungodly hour. I think I went to bed at 4.

Jake: We went in there and we sat together and waited.

Jeni: It was family court, so there were custody hearings and parents in absolute distress, and lots of people crying and just looking so angry. And here we were hungover from our divorce party, hanging out together and probably bantering under our breath. We were last on the docket. So, we had to sit through all of this super sad, depressing stuff, before we got to our divorce hearing.

Jake: Finally, the judge said, "I need one of you to take the stand." And I looked at Jeni and she's like, you go. And I was like, yeah, that sounds alright. I'll go.

Jeni: So, you know, she [the judge] went through all the questions that you have to ask, are you both in agreement? Blah, blah, blah. And then at the very end, she says, Mr. and Mrs. Fleming, will you please approach the bench? And I thought the only reason I know what that means is because I've seen it on TV. So, we walked up there right in front of her, and she said to us: "I've been a fan of your music for 10 years. I really love what you do. And it's not often that I get to preside over such an amicable divorce. And I hope that this means that you guys will continue to make music together." It was a big deal for the judge to go out of her way for a couple who just got divorced. We were appreciative of those words.

Jake: It was a huge affirmation. Yeah.

Jeni: After the hearing, we went out to breakfast with a couple of friends and a bottle of champagne. And we knew the waiter pretty well, and asked him, "Hey, can you pop this bottle of champagne for us?" And he says, "Oh sure, what's the special occasion?" And Jake and I said, "We just got divorced" and the look on his face went blank, but like a second later, he says, "That's great!" And he poured a glass for himself. And we all toasted at the table. And it was the weirdest, most bizarre breakfast scene.

Jake: It was like the universe itself saying, "This relationship isn't over—it just has a new shape."

Jeni: And that's exactly what happened. We continued to play music together, even if we had to step back from some of our joint projects at first. Other bands, cover groups, those were easier to navigate emotionally, and they allowed our musical collaboration to continue without complicating the divorce.

Jake: Our friendship and musical partnership stayed strong, and that gave us both freedom to move into new chapters.

Jeni: Right. Jake fell in love again, and I felt genuinely happy for him. It wasn't about jealousy or regret—it was about seeing him find joy and fulfillment. And when his daughter, Betty, was born, I felt love for her too, almost like an honorary aunt.

Jake: And I think that's the most beautiful part of all this: love transforms, it doesn't disappear. Our relationship didn't end with the divorce. We love each other more now in a different, freer way.

Jeni: We really do. And we also want people to know that you can design your divorce your way. It doesn't have to be destructive, bitter, or expensive. You can keep respect, keep collaboration, keep love—even if your life together changes completely.

Jake: And celebrate it! A divorce party, a shared meal, music, laughter—it's about moving forward consciously and joyfully.

Jeni: Yes. Divorce doesn't have to erase history; it can honor it while opening space for new beginnings. And for us, it led to continued music, continued friendship, and continued love—for each other and for our families.

Jake: That's the good divorce.

Jeni: That's the one worth having.

CHAPTER THREE

THE BREAKUP

REFLECTION: THE GREAT UNRAVELING

That evening, after we put Anya and Dwyer to bed, David and I sat down on our well-worn couch, with its fabric beginning to fray around the corners and its springs going flat from the bounce of tiny feet. The house was quiet, except for the refrigerator's hum and the purr of the kittens who curled up with us.

I finally spoke the words that nobody ever wants to speak, "So, is this it? Are we done?"

David sighed. "'Poorly married,'" he quoted. "Yeah, I guess we're done." We reached for each other's hand because, why wouldn't we? That's what felt most natural. Shifting from "fight for our marriage" to "fight each other" wasn't a light switch moment; it was more like a dimmer switch. Did we have to fight each other? Couldn't we just skip that part, and instead fight for a good divorce?

I felt the prickle of tears in my eyes, and then the floodgates suddenly opened. I wanted him to wrap his arms around me and comfort me, like he had done hundreds of times before. But now there was a new invisible boundary that had sprung up between us.

Instead, he stood up from the couch. "I'll sleep downstairs tonight," he offered, not looking at me.

I thought about all the nights stretching ahead of us—the separate beds, the separate homes, the dividing of holidays and weekends, the complicated logistics of becoming two households instead of one. It felt overwhelming— this massive change we were about to undertake was just too much.

"No," I implored. "Come to bed. Just for tonight. Like you have every night before. Everything is going to change so quickly. Just ... not tonight. That feels too hard." I could feel the sadness coming off of me in waves. The whole time we were fighting to save our marriage, I was frustrated, stressed, and exhausted—but I hadn't felt grief. It was new.

He nodded. We went through our bedtime routine in silence—brushing our teeth, washing our faces, and slipping into the sheets. The familiar choreography felt different now, tinged with the knowledge that we were performing it for the last time.

As we laid in bed, with a careful distance between us, my head was spinning. Halloween was around the corner; how would we trick or treat with the kids? Where will we all live? How much is this going to cost us? Would we be together on Christmas morning? How could we possibly tell the kids? To say that I was spiraling was an understatement.

Our marriage was ending, but not our relationship, and certainly not our family.

THE LEAD-UP TO THE GREAT UNRAVELING

"Come on kids, let's get going, it's late," I hollered down the length of the hallway, absent of patience. It had been a long day. David and I had a therapy session earlier, I was swamped at work, and we ate dinner later than normal. David had a late-night work commitment and had to rush out, leaving the cleanup and bedtime tasks to me. I wasn't at my best going into bedtime that night. It only got worse from there.

I was already brewing with resentment over the usual annoyances, which seemed to grow in size daily. I was disappointed about not being better at married life. We were trying to shelter Anya and Dwyer from our marital problems and the bickering that came along with them. At times, our struggles escalated and our yelling was at full volume, with us believing that the kids didn't really notice. We could not have been more wrong.

Anya was making Dwyer laugh by dropping an octopus bath toy from the top of her reach and letting it splash in the bath water. Anya did this repeatedly, and Dwyer's delight only encouraged her to keep going. All I could think about was how wound up they would be—it would take ages to get them calmed down and into bed. They were also making yet another mess I would have to clean up. At first it was just a little splash. But then Anya wanted a bigger laugh out of Dwyer, so the pink octopus was being dunked under the water with force. In his excitement, Dwyer picked up a toy and did the same. Water was sloshing around the bathtub, as the two wriggled in the water and laughed into their bellies. All I could see was the problem at hand and a mess to clean up.

"Stop splashing!" I said, grabbing for a towel to sop up a puddle. But they didn't stop fast enough for me. "Anya! Dwyer! I said, stop it right NOW. You are ruining the house!" My voice had an edge to it, with my pent-up anger seeping through, and it was loud enough to scare my small children.

Anya and Dwyer froze mid-splash. It took me a second to realize how I'd acted. Their eyes were so wide, and their shoulders were up around their ears, bodies tense and afraid of what I might do next. My children were afraid of me, and it wasn't the first time. This kind of outburst was becoming more common; it was gutting me and wounding my children.

Their faces took the wind out of me.

"Oh, honey," I said, dropping the towel, and reaching to gently touch their pink cheeks in reassurance. "I'm so sorry—I didn't mean to yell. I'm sorry. You're okay. The house is okay. I'm okay," but I knew things were not okay.

The person I was becoming in this marriage—short-tempered, constantly exhausted, emotionally volatile—was not the mother I wanted to be for my children or the wife my husband deserved. Despite my love for our family, I was turning into someone I didn't recognize or like.

Was "staying for the kids" valid if I was becoming a worse mother by staying in my marriage?

Maybe I needed to *leave* for my kids.

ROCK AND A HARD PLACE

Part of what makes us so bad at breakups is our general tendency to avoid them. There are plenty of reasons to stay, and it's less clear why we should go. We feel like we need a "justifiable" reason. And sometimes, that reason isn't obvious.

Researchers have found that children are actually harmed more by high-conflict homes than by divorce itself. The traditional wisdom of "staying together for the kids" has been challenged by studies showing that children exposed to chronic parental conflict—even when it's not openly hostile—experience higher levels of anxiety, depression, and behavior problems than children whose parents separate amicably. Also, some studies suggest that children in high-conflict intact families may fare as badly or worse in certain dimensions compared to children whose parents divorce but minimize conflict.[1]

What matters most isn't whether parents stay married, but whether they can provide a stable, loving environment. I often tell my clients that divorce alone doesn't damage kids. Whether married or unmarried, adults behaving badly damages kids. Yet, given the unsavory option of divorce, it's no wonder that couples choose to stick it out, do more damage, and pass by the clearly marked exit.

Two people often get so caught up in their conflict with each other, it leaves little room for anything else. With constant tension in the home (or in some cases, constantly avoiding each other), each person becomes a more stressed version of themselves. As a result, the relationship becomes all work and no fun. Where is the ease? I'm not saying healthy relationships should be easy. I'm saying there should be ease in the relationship.

---

[1] Morrison, D. R. and Coiro, M. J. (1999). Parental conflict and marital disruption: do children benefit when high-conflict marriages are dissolved? *Journal of Marriage and the Family* 61(3), 626–637. https://doi.org/10.2307/353565.

PARTNERED

Our culture is saturated with myths about romantic love that shape our expectations of relationships in profound ways. We're taught that finding "the one" will solve our problems, fill our emptiness, and give our lives meaning. Modern fairy tales suggest that the right partner should complete us, be our "better half." We absorb the message that our life's happiness hinges on finding one magical person who will understand our quirks and fulfill all our needs.

In her 2006 book, *Mating in Captivity*, psychotherapist Esther Perel challenges the common thinking around marriage, "Today, we turn to one person to provide what an entire village once did: a sense of grounding, meaning, and continuity. At the same time, we expect our committed relationships to be romantic as well as emotionally and sexually fulfilling. Is it any wonder that so many relationships crumble under the weight of it all?"[2]

Besides setting false expectations when entering relationships, these myths can make leaving romantic relationships difficult too. You're publicly committing yourself to one romantic partner for life. And it's rightfully a big sign of commitment, often more so than living together or having a child together. Marriage is legally binding. A legal contract most of us don't understand when we say, "I do." Most people, even knowing the likelihood of divorce, still marry, telling themselves, "That will never be us." And if they have internalized any of the modern myths about marriage (and relationships more generally), divorcing can be even harder to do.

As a relationship deepens, we feel more attached. Even spending more time together can create a bond. Humans feel safe in consistency. So even when a relationship is tumultuous, we may stay because it's at least familiar. And if we believe the person completes us, we might be even more tempted

---

[2] Perel, E. (2006). *Mating in captivity: reconciling the erotic and the domestic.* HarperCollins.

to stick it out, in the hopes that the situation will improve. Society reinforces this, celebrating couples who stick it out "through thick and thin" while stigmatizing divorce as a failure. Maybe it's no longer a moral failure, but it's still evidence that someone made a (big) mistake.

There is also the economics of "sunk costs" to consider, which suggests that once we have invested in something (whether a relationship or a financial investment), we stay in it so that the costs (e.g. effort, time, or money) aren't wasted. Sunk costs sound logical when looking to the past. But looking only at the sunk costs means you're discounting the effort, time, or money required in the future to maintain the investment. Subscribing to sunk costs makes us forget that the relationship, if going poorly now, may not improve, despite how much it has cost us in the past.

After investing years in a partnership—building a home, possibly raising children, and intertwining finances and social circles—the prospect of walking away doesn't seem logical. We can't get back the years we dated someone. We can't get back the years we spent fighting with a spouse. We can mistakenly think that the fighting is worth it, if we figure it out and stay together. But it's also possible the arguing continues. It's possible your relationship stays parked in some purgatorial lot, never reaching a new destination.

Some people might struggle to leave a relationship because they can't envision what life would be like without their partner. Even if from the outside, others may recognize the improvements that could be made. Yet, when you are in a relationship, it can be difficult to see out of it for a variety of reasons. Some couples simply succumb to staying together, because they wouldn't know how to be apart.

The psychology of connection keeps us in relationships longer than logic might dictate. Our brains release neurochemicals (like oxytocin and dopamine) that bond us to our partners and make separation physically and emotionally painful. This attachment system developed long ago to keep our ancestors close to their tribes and committed to raising their young. But in modern relationships, it can trap people in unhealthy dynamics and expose kids to high-conflict environments.

Our nervous system responds to the potential loss of a significant relationship as if we're in physical danger, triggering fight, flight, or freeze responses that keep us stuck in unhealthy patterns. These biological realities help explain why people often tolerate behaviors and situations they never would accept from a friend or colleague, simply because the thought of breaking the attachment is too terrifying to contemplate.

The term *conscious uncoupling* was first published in the 2009 book *Conscious Uncoupling: 5 Steps to Living Happily Even After* by Katherine Woodward Thomas. The phrase gained widespread public recognition in 2014, when Gwyneth Paltrow used it to announce her split from Chris Martin. David and I would have benefited greatly from Thomas's framework, had we known about it. Her primary principles—acknowledging deeper emotions beyond conflict, finding healthy ways to release resentment, setting intentions for the future relationship—provide needed stability during the rupture of the old relationship.

Thomas reminds us that the pain and torment of a breakup should not be underestimated. She writes, "You have nowhere to hide. Life has broken you open and it is violently, mercilessly forcing you to evolve, to develop, and to grow," emphasizing that the intense emotions following a separation, while difficult, can also serve as a catalyst for personal growth and self-discovery. She writes, "In a nutshell, a breakup is nothing short of a once-in-a-lifetime opportunity to have a complete spiritual awakening. One that catapults you to a whole new level of authenticity, compassion, wisdom, depth, and—dare I say it?—even joy."[3]

---

[3] Thomas, Katherine Woodward. (2016). Conscious uncoupling: 5 steps to living happily even after. Harmony.

PACKING THE PARACHUTE

For years before we made the decision to divorce, I found myself thinking about practical matters: Where would I live if David and I separated? How would we handle finances? Could either of us afford to live alone? I heard about "nesting" arrangements where children stay in the family home while parents rotate in and out. In the end, I simply felt paralyzed.

I was, in effect, packing my psychological parachute, preparing for a jump I wasn't yet ready to make. I realize now this is a common pattern. We often know in our hearts when a relationship is over, long before we're ready to act on that knowledge. I was collecting information, making small preparations, mentally rehearsing my exit, all while outwardly maintaining the status quo, hoping I wouldn't have to pull the ripcord.

As my marriage continued to deteriorate despite our efforts, I found myself seeking alternative relationship models. I kept my eyes and ears alert, for examples of divorced couples who were doing things differently, better. I sought out people who had managed to end their marriages without becoming enemies or traumatizing their children.

One day at Anya's gymnastics class, I was sitting in the viewing gallery, making small talk with the other parents and grandparents. My long-time friend Jacki wasn't there to pick up her son, so her mother Rebecca was doing grandma-Uber duty. Rebecca had divorced Jacki's father decades ago, but I knew from Jacki that as adults the whole family was often together: both of her parents and her stepdad. In fact, her dad and stepdad are pretty chummy and are known for long card matches during family gatherings. This sounded dreamy to me. I wondered how she managed that. I couldn't shake the thought from my brain that maybe there was such a thing as a *good divorce*.

As we watched the children tumble on the mats, I scooted a bit closer to Rebecca and struck up a conversation. After the typical chatter about the weather and our little people performing flips in front of us, I prodded her about divorce.

"You know," I said, "I've always been impressed by your family, and how everyone gets along, in spite of the divorce. That seems rare. Do you see it that way?"

Rebecca tilted her head and looked at me curiously, "Well," she began, turning back to watch her grandson and the other kids, "Over time, you begin to realize that all the crap you were holding onto really doesn't matter. At the end of the day, we are still a family, and we are going to be in each other's orbit forever. So, we decided to speed up the time machine and get to the good stuff as soon as possible." She paused, thinking. "But it still took time to heal from the divorce and find a new path. Time is an extraordinary elixir of healing that really can't be replaced by anything else, but you can hit the gas pedal and help it along—if you're smart."

She went on to explain how she and her first husband negotiated their new relationship carefully, putting their kids' needs first but also respecting each other's boundaries. They could be in the same room without tension. They celebrated holidays together when it made sense, and separately when it didn't. They were outwardly flexible and kind, even when it was difficult.

"Whenever things got tense, I tried to remember what was important, and all the love I have for our kids. I did care about him and wanted the best for him, still do. I just didn't want to be married to him anymore—that part didn't work," she replied. "The marriage ended, but our family was still our family. We still had kids to raise, memories to honor, and a future to build together."

"You make it sound so easy," feeling my face flush, hoping she wouldn't notice my grasping for hope behind the thin veil of my faltering marriage.

"We weren't perfect at it," she admitted. Then, she turned to me and smiled. "There were hard days. But we tried our best to do it with grace."

DIVORCE CURIOUS

I found myself eavesdropping in cafes, restaurants, and parks anytime I got a whiff of a divorce conversation taking place. Some stories gave me hope, like my musician friends who had a Marriage Completion party to announce their divorce. Fifteen years later, they can still be found sharing a stage and making music together—even with new partners in their life.

There were also plenty of stories that terrified me. One woman burst into tears when speaking with a confidante about the custody battle that she was embroiled in with her ex. Another woman cackled with a group of women as she discussed her new dating life. A man with dark hair continually sighed as (presumably) his mother prodded him about his separation. Another dad hung his head with the weight of a judicial system that seemed to have a very strong mom-bias.

David's parents divorced when he was a senior in high school. I saw his family as an inspiring and positive model. The first time I met his mom and her second husband at a large family gathering, his dad was also there. Like most people, I was surprised to see them all together having a jolly time. No drama, no awkward tension, just grown-ups enjoying their family together. Why should this kind of scene surprise any of us? We have been so brainwashed as a culture to believe divorce is synonymous with enemy warfare. We have lost our imagination for families transcending divorce together.

DO NO HARM

Over the past seven months, I had made the commute from our home to Fort Missoula so many times it had become a ritual. A ritual that starts the moment I wake up on *Therapy Day*; a day of dread, hope, anxiety, panic, calm, confusion, and clarity. That pretty much sums up couples counseling. Today was different, however. Today, it felt like a storm cloud full of lightning right over my head, casting dark shadows and rumbling with a sense of dread. The old officer's row of buildings stood like sentinels against the mountain backdrop, their white stucco facades glowing in the autumn light. The broad, bold front porch that had once been filled with our wedding guests, laughing, eating, and celebrating our union, now mocked my arrival.

David was sitting in the chair-made-for-one when I opened the heavy front door.

"Hi," I said, trying to gently engage, but cautious of emotional landmines, as they seemed to be hiding everywhere these days. The slightest exhale in the wrong direction could set off an explosion, for either of us. He'd been sleeping downstairs in the guest room and left early for a meeting, so I hadn't seen him yet that day.

We had begun to put the kids to bed and then go our separate ways and into separate bedrooms. In the morning, we would reverse the ritual, so the kids wouldn't start asking questions, "Where's Daddo?," "Why is Daddo sleeping downstairs?" Until we knew what we were doing, there was no need to get the kids involved, and we certainly weren't ready to tell them. We had been pretending for months that everything was fine. We could pretend a little longer.

The weekend had been full of kids' activities and domestic chores, so we hadn't talked much about the divorce yet. I was sort of hoping this bonus session with Esther would provide some guidance on how to talk about it going forward. We were both so tired and sad, dealing with our own grief since we'd made the decision. It still felt very surreal, and I was questioning myself constantly. This thing that I wanted, this thing I thought would make things better, is clearly going to make things so much harder. But for how long? Could I endure the time away from my children that was going to be required of me? Would we each financially land on our feet? Would our kids take a downward spiral?

Esther's office occupied the main floor of the large home. The waiting room was empty when we entered. But almost immediately, she appeared in the hallway, thankfully. This wasn't a day I could endure a long wait in the heaviness of our silence.

"Karen, David, come on in," she said, with a gentle smile. We stood up and made our way down the hallway, keeping a careful distance between us. Not close enough to suggest unity, not far enough to imply hostility. Just two people navigating the strange choreography of coming apart.

We followed her into the room. I chose the chair instead of the couch, and David sat at the far end of the couch, his posture stiff. What happened next seemed less important than what would happen after. Where would we go from here? How would we untangle so many years of a shared life and the forever-result of entangling our DNA? The sheer logistics of divorce loomed before me like a mountain too steep to climb. Like most couples arriving at this threshold, we didn't know what we were doing or where to begin.

"So," Esther began, settling into her chair. "A decision has been made, a very hard decision. How are you doing at home?" She looked at each of us in turn. It seemed like an impossible question to answer. "Have you told the children?"

"No. God no. We don't know what to tell them, or how to tell them, or when, or where. We don't know anything." There was panic in my voice. The fear of screwing up our kids surged through me every day.

"Well, I don't have much to offer you on this side of your decision." Her words landed with a thud in my heart. "You will need to contact lawyers to do the legal part. I believe there is a self-help legal center at the courthouse. You might be able to get some of the paperwork there. I think they also have volunteer lawyers or paralegals from the law school who pop in a few hours each week."

That was it? This was all she had to offer, to call lawyers? I knew lawyers could get us divorced, but who was going to teach us how to *be* divorced? I didn't know it then, but this was the moment seeds were planted for what would become the Good Divorce Academy. The mantra in my head was screaming out: *We need someone to show us HOW to do this really hard and important thing. We need an education. We need help, guidance, and support. We need more than a legal document.*

She must have seen the frustration and despair in my face. "I have a couple of things you can consider as you move forward. First, do no more harm. I suspect enough harm has already been done. No need for more. This applies to every conversation, text message, words passed between the two of you. Even how you speak about each other in public and certainly how you speak about each other in front of your children. Your work now is to protect your future, your children's future, the future of your family." She leaned in, "Every decision you make from this point forward should pass through this filter: *Will this hurt my children?* If the answer is yes, find another way."

We both nodded in agreement. However, we would find this to be more difficult than anticipated. When emotions are high and feelings are raw, all sorts of regrettable things can come flying out of one's mouth. Even the subtle eye roll or annoyed exhale gives way to resentment and contempt winning the day.

"Second," Esther continued, "your goal is to become indifferent toward each other."

I shifted on the couch. "What exactly do you mean by that?" I asked.

"Right now, you both have intense feelings about each other—anger, hurt, disappointment, maybe even resentment at times," Esther explained. "The goal isn't to suddenly become best friends. It's to reach a place when seeing each other, or hearing each other's name, doesn't trigger an emotional response. Where you can coexist without those wounds reopening. The trigger points become less and less tender. This will be a gift to your nervous system and your future relationship."

Okay ..., I thought. *This seems impossible.* I couldn't imagine being void of feelings about David. He was the father of my children. I would always care for him. I had so many giant feelings about this man coursing through my nervous system all the time.

"And finally," Esther said, her voice softening, "remember that while your marriage is ending, your relationship is not. You will always be connected through your children. You'll share graduations, weddings, grandchildren—all of life's significant moments. The nature of your relationship is changing, but it will continue for the rest of your lives. You have a forever relationship, what do you want it to look like?"

I nodded at all the right moments, made the appropriate sounds of agreement, even wrote some notes down to think about later. But inside, skepticism and confusion battled with the rational part of my brain.

As I sat there listening to Esther, I kept coming back to her first tenet: do no more harm. How was that even possible? We were about to split our family in two, disrupt our children's sense of security, and force them to shuttle between homes through their entire childhood. Wasn't that the definition of harm? We were already going ahead with the thing that would hurt them most—the divorce itself.

And becoming indifferent toward David? I almost laughed out loud at the thought. We'd spent the last eight years in and out of therapy precisely because we weren't indifferent. We loved, we fought, we cried, we tried to fix things—indifference would have been a blessing. You don't spend thousands of dollars on marriage counselors when you feel *indifferent*. Our problem wasn't too much indifference; it was too much of everything else: disappointment, resentment, hurt, even love. The thought of emotionally detaching from my husband would be like trying to untangle an old vine from its post.

The only tenet that made any sense was the last one—that our relationship would continue, albeit transformed. We would always be Anya and Dwyer's parents. We would always share that history, those memories. No one in the world would ever understand the deep love I carry for my children more than David, because he carries that same deep love.

What would this new relationship look like? Would we be like those divorced couples who can barely stand to be in the same room during parent-teacher conferences? Or worse yet, be like those parents who can't even endure the same conference and have to schedule separate ones with the teacher? Would our children be required to divide their day of Christmas magic in half, changing out of candy cane pajamas at noon to pack up their new special toys and relocate, just so life would be equal according to the parenting plan? Would we be able to sit as a family at the school choir concert, or would our children have to dart their eyes around the bleachers in search of their dispersed fan club? Maybe we could forge something better, something good. Or at least good enough.

FOREVER

"Your marriage is ending, but not your relationship." At first, this seemed like an empty platitude, a therapist's attempt to soften the blow of divorce. But as we navigated those early weeks and months, I began to understand the truth in her words. We weren't severing all ties; we were transforming our connection. Our relationship as romantic partners was ending, but our relationship as co-parents would remain. It was time to renovate our parenting relationship, not destroy it.

We both worked toward minimizing harm. The time for blame had passed, it seemed. The more I thought about alternative approaches to divorce, the more determined I was to discover something different for our family. I rejected the adversarial approach encouraged by the divorce industry. David and I had failed at marriage, but we didn't have to fail at divorce. We could choose a different path, one that honored what our relationship had been, while creating space for what it would become.

I was slowly grappling with the understanding that divorce calls us to transform and restructure our family and our co-parent relationship. I was hopeful that, like his own family, David and I could be cordial enough to eventually have family dinners or holidays together. I still held on to ideas of being a family who just didn't live together. I refused to adopt the moniker of "broken family." In those early days of separation, we fumbled through the practical and emotional complexities. But we also laid the groundwork for the good divorce I longed for.

Esther's three tenets became our guiding principles:

- Do no more harm.
- Work toward indifference.
- You have a forever relationship.

These simple directives helped us navigate difficult moments and make decisions that served our family's long-term well-being. When we disagreed about schedules or possessions, I would return to these principles, asking myself which choice would cause the least harm to our children, and which would foster the kind of post-marriage relationship I hoped to build. I failed frequently, still do, and have regrets. I like to think that my improvement rate generally trends upwards. I'm in a constant state of practicing, not perfecting.

Together, we set intentions for our future relationship. We wanted our children to see us treating each other with respect and kindness. We wanted to attend Anya's piano recitals and Dwyer's baseball games without creating tension. We wanted to be able to share holidays and special occasions without the drama that often accompanies divorced families. Most importantly, we wanted our children to feel that their family, though restructured, remained intact—that they weren't losing anything essential by having parents who lived apart. We would be there—kindergarten to college, graduation to grandbabies, forever.

IN THEIR OWN WORDS

The Good Divorce Show
Season 1, Episode11
Mercedes
Married 10 years, 2 sons (8 and 10)
Remarried 14 years

Listen to the full episode here:

ONE BIG HAPPY FAMILY

Karen:　When we head off to the courthouse to get married, it's probably one or two pages of paperwork and lickety-split it's done.

Mercedes:　Totally easy to get married. Yes. So easy.

Karen:　But it's really complex to get unmarried.

Mercedes:　Yes. And honestly, it just gave me such a bad vibe. When I realized that Raul was going to be told what he had to pay in child support, and they were going to require me to set up visitations, well I was never going to do that. Money and paying for things was never an issue with Raul ever. And I was never going to prevent our kids from seeing him whenever he wanted to see them, and vice versa. It was clear a traditional divorce just wasn't for us.

So, Raul and I looked at the paperwork and at each other, and I said, "Well, what do you want to do?" And he said, "Are you planning on getting married or anything like that? I mean, is that in your mindset here?" And I said, "No, not at all. What about you?" And he responded, "I will never get married again, period." And I said, "Well, you know, as my mother used to say, 'You never can always sometimes tell,' her way of saying *never say never*, just in case."

Karen: We've done that one before.

Mercedes: ....more than once! At this point, we both agreed that this was silly and to just let it go. We'll wait until the kids are over 18 and then get legally divorced. So, we just didn't care about it anymore. And it made it so much easier.

So, we sold the house. I do remember having a conversation with the boys a little bit. I think they kind of knew what was going on. But we made it sound exactly the way it was: yes, we are separating. Yes, we will be living in separate households. But we are family. We will always be family. We're mom and dad. And you don't have anything to worry about.

They were about 10 and 8. They didn't have questions. They didn't seem worried about anything. Raul and I were best buddies. We were joking around, and everything was just fine. And I want to be clear because somebody asked me this once before: were you really like siblings? I absolutely promise you, we were romantically as dead as dead could be. No monkey business of any kind. We were truly family, and that was it.

So, then the question came: where are we moving to? How about an apartment? Raul agreed, "Do we want to get an apartment where the two doors are right next to each other?" I responded, "No, maybe that's a little too close." So, we found two apartment complexes that had a tennis court between them. I rented in one of the complexes and he rented in the other. And the boys could just cross the tennis court to go back and forth.

Karen: I'm going to ask a couple of clarifying questions, because I think this is a fascinating arrangement. If you were getting along so well and you wanted to raise your kids in close proximity, why did you even separate? How did you know this was the right choice for your family?

Mercedes: Because there's a difference between being friends and being husband and wife. There's a romantic part. There's a sexual part. And that was dead for us. We still had the chance to grow in those areas with other people (or not). We weren't that couple anymore, but we were still the same family we've always been.

Karen: Was there ever a parenting schedule?

Mercedes: Nope. Raul's greatest pain with the separation was knowing he wouldn't be living with the kids anymore. He had total free reign to come in and out of my apartment, because I had made the decision from the get-go that no other man or potential love interest would ever be there. My home was our primary family home. Always safe, always available, just for the four of us. Raul could come and go, be with the kids, eat together, horse around with them, put them to bed. You know, the typical stuff parents share with their children. We always knew where the kids were and each other. It was very natural and easy-going for us. Raul never abused that freedom either. I could easily say, "Not tonight" or "Why don't you and the kids go do something outside of the home, so I can do something for myself." Again, easy.

Karen: Did they have bedrooms in both apartments?

Mercedes: No. They had their rooms with me. Raul rented a one-bedroom apartment, so if they slept there it was on the couch. I had a three-bedroom apartment.

Karen: And that was their permanent home.

Mercedes: Absolutely. And I could count on him so much, that within the first year I met somebody out of state, and we started dating long distance. He was a pilot and he had a private chartering company. So, I started flying back and forth, and you know, just having a lot of fun. And Raul loved it because when I was gone, he could stay at my apartment with the kids. Oh, he loved that, because that was his opportunity to be with them, to wake up with them, to be the dad 24/7.

The boys lived with me and would go up the road to see their father anytime they wanted. Raul came over frequently. It was like, "Hey, I got some steaks. Do you want me to cook them?" I loved it when he would cook. We could still be a family without having to be married or coupled, without drama. We created this loving and dedicated family dynamic that was just wonderful for all of us. Like married but not married.

Karen: We're wrapping our heads around that one.

Mercedes: I know.

Karen: This gives us an imagination for what a family can look like.

Mercedes: It's a wonderful thing. Raul is my 3 a.m. phone call. He has my best interest at heart.

Karen: You were never going to amputate their father from their life.

Mercedes: I would never even consider it. Why would I hurt all these people?

Karen: Divorce isn't what damages children. It's adults behaving badly that damages children. Married or not married, the responsibility rests with the parents.

Mercedes: Absolutely. It wasn't a divorce for our family; it was a realignment. You're getting out of the couplehood and turning it into something else. In my case, that something else was even better. I couldn't ask for a better relationship with Raul. There is still an element of '*til death do us part.*

Karen: You co-mingled your DNA. That's forever.

Mercedes: Yes, forever. We each started to do some dating and could easily share those things, like siblings. I think that came naturally for us because we remained very close, but the coupling aspect of us was no more. It was completely dead. We truly felt nothing for each other in that department, which allowed us to be indifferent when it came to dating others. No lingering baggage, no resentments, just no negative feelings of any kind. He had a few girlfriends over the years. One of them wanted him to move to San Francisco and Raul wouldn't do that. Family comes first for him. Another girlfriend was extremely jealous. He couldn't share a birthday with his sons and me without constant disruptions, so he cut that short. From that experience, relationships were kind of light for him, and that's the way he wanted it.

I, on the other hand, was extremely lucky. I had just started a new relationship at a distance with Tom. He was in Michigan. We used to go to elementary school together, and he found me 40 years later on Facebook. At around the same time, Raul developed some health issues. He was in great pain and could not work. My sons had already moved to Houston, so I was an empty nester. What was the right thing to do? For me, it was to help him. He needed us.

I remember calling Tom at the time and explaining the problem. "Tom, I know this is a little odd, but Raul needs to come live here with me while he is going through this health issue. He can't even walk to the bathroom. It's likely going to take months. Are you ok with that?" Tom said, "Of course, don't even think about it, just do it!" So, Raul moved in with me after the kids were gone.

It takes special people to enter a family like ours, where exes are family and Tom was that guy. Fourteen years later and still going strong. Tom and Raul became "brothers from a different mother," as they like to say, but that's a different story for another time.

CHAPTER FOUR

THE KIDS

REFLECTION: HAVING THE TALK

In all my years of reciting lines and speaking in front of an audience, the hardest talk I ever gave was in our living room, with two small spectators who mattered more than any audience I'd ever face.

When it was time to tell our children, I knew I'd need (and want) to think about what we were going to say before we had to say it. I didn't want to bumble through this, say the wrong thing, or do irreversible damage. The goal was to comfort them as we simultaneously began to tear their world apart. How to do it was a daunting mystery.

One evening after the kids were asleep, David and I once again sat at the kitchen counter, facing more divorce business. I held a legal pad for comfort, hoping the words that would forever change our family would magically appear on the page. We were navigating unknown territory and hoping our instincts would show the way. By the end of the night, the yellow pages of the legal pad were splotched with tears and empty words.

We had an outline complete with who would start the conversation and who would wrap up. What came in between those moments was nebulous and dependent on the kids' reactions. Our kids were only five and six years old, so finding the age-appropriate language was important. Did they even have an understanding of divorce? Would they cry? Get angry? Run out of the room?

I was filled with guilt, concern, and fear. At the same time, I dreaded the conversation and also wanted to get it over with, so I could stop thinking about it constantly. The nights were restless, sleep was elusive, and my days filled with fog of the unknown. It was hard to keep pretending around the house that everything was business as usual. My mind whirred, wondering if I could manage to navigate the conversation without totally breaking down. It seemed important that I keep it together, so my kids wouldn't feel the need to comfort me or follow my emotional lead.

I waffled between feeling incredibly guilty for what I was about to do, and sturdy in my conviction that divorce was what our family needed. The curtain was about to rise on our new family structure. The script was written. The stage was set. Now we just needed the courage to deliver our lines.

We decided to chat with the kids on a Friday after school, so they would have the weekend to process, adjust, ask questions, or do whatever they needed. It was all very unpredictable; I was grateful to have the safety net of our outline. At least we talked before the talk. After school, we gathered as a family on the couch. Dwyer snuggled up on my lap, as Anya sat between David and me.

"Anya, Dwyer," I began, "You know we love you very much."

"So much," David chimed in. Both of us are trying to push through the lump in our throats.

"And we want to tell you"—my breath momentarily caught and I cleared my throat. "We're going to have two houses for our family, instead of one." I couldn't even utter the word divorce.

"I'm going to be in a new home," David said, "and Mama will stay in this home. And you'll live with both of us, in both homes."

Anya frowned, revealing the familiar furrow in her brow, and tilted her head ever so slightly to the side. Dwyer, at five years old, just swung his little legs, the heel of his foot rhythmically hitting the couch.

"We are getting a divorce." I figured I better just name it, "That means Daddo and I are going to live apart."

"A divorce," came Anya's voice, trying to comprehend the truth that had just landed. "A divorce" she said again and then tears began to stream down her sweet little cheeks as she wrapped her arms around her Daddo.

"It's going to be okay, don't you worry about a thing," David said comforting Anya and mentally trying to believe his own words. It was unclear if Dwyer was able to grasp the consequence of the situation. "You are going to have lots of time with both of us, and we will always be with you for all the important stuff."

At the moment, it didn't seem we needed to say anything more, or that we even should. The announcement was enough to absorb, and we didn't want to overwhelm them. I'm famous for saying too many words for too long, so we made the strategic pivot to distract.

David chimed in, "And we have a surprise for your bedroom at your new home."

Dwyer's face immediately lit up in anticipation of a present, unable to fully grasp the weight of the message. Anya remained weepy and curled up on David's lap.

"What is it?" Dwyer asked.

"It's in the garage—would you like to see it?" I replied.

The pair looked at each other and then nodded at us.

We walked them from the living room out to the garage where a new set of bunk beds awaited. They both gasped in excitement. These bunk beds were even more special than the current set. These were made of wood and had a built-in desk. Forever the protector of her little brother, Anya claimed the top bunk, saying, "You're too little to be on top Dwyer. And I will need the desk for all my art supplies and homework."

It worked; the distraction in the garage moved them out of the conversation and into a new vision. David and I looked at each other through glistening eyes, holding back a flood of sadness, straddling the impossible crevasse of grief and relief.

Once the excitement started to wane, Anya had many questions, most notably the timing of everything to come. We went back inside and showed the two of them the calendar we marked up with the schedule for the next couple of weeks. It showed the timing for David's move-out date and the forever-change from our single-family home to becoming a 2Home Family.

Anya has anxious tendencies and likes to know what to expect. I knew a schedule would comfort her. She took that calendar, tacked it up next to her bed, and crossed out every day until they would have their first overnight at their new house, which was about 10 days down the road. The schedule provided some sense of control when things felt out of control.

We walked them through the days they would stay at each home: two nights with me, then two nights with Dad. The thought of it gutted me. I was about to relinquish half of all bedtime stories. Half of the morning snuggles. Half of the magical moments of new discoveries. Half, half, half—divorce is dominated by division. It's painful math, no matter how you look at it.

HOW WE BEGIN IS OFTEN HOW WE END

As a divorce consultant, I have ushered other families through their own impossible moments of having "The Talk." I remind them, "This is an indelible conversation. Everyone will remember the details and carry those details with them into adulthood. It is essential to consider not just the words, but also the timing and location of the conversation." It is one of the most important and often glossed-over steps in the divorce process; how we begin is often how we end.

A podcast guest recalled her mom blurting out the news from behind the steering wheel of the car, on Ninth Avenue, on the way home from Girl Scouts, "Your dad and I are getting a divorce; you are going to live mostly with me." She was nine years old at the time, holding onto her little sister in the backseat. My guest shared the details of the story on the podcast, as if it had just happened last week, and not 40 years prior.

Another parent, while negotiating yet another argument over breakfast with their spouse, turned to the kids, who were quietly finishing their pancakes, "I can't take it anymore. I'm divorcing your dad. There, now you know!," leaving a wake of shock and despair as she stormed out of the kitchen.

With intention and attention, these traumatic moments can be avoided.

THE GOOD GUIDE: FINDING THE WORDS

Remember, this is not a time for your kids to comfort you. Try to keep it together. Showing emotion is appropriate; this is a hard and sad truth you are sharing. But if you completely fall apart, not only will that set the tone for the kids' response, but they may also feel they need to come to your rescue. This conversation is not about you; your job is to comfort your children, not the other way around.

For my children, it was important they knew we would always love them and take care of them, as that wasn't changing. As their parents, David and I wanted to make things better, not worse. That's the point of divorce after all—to make a not-so-great thing better. Our children needed to hear that our decision had nothing to do with them.

Here are a few general guidelines to help with your own impossible conversation.

1. **WHEN will the conversation happen?**
   a. **Context:** Consider other activities or special events that might be happening around the same time (e.g. sporting events, birthday parties, holidays, vacations, etc.) and try to navigate around them. No one wants to hear that their parents are getting a divorce and then have to dash off to a soccer game.
   b. **Window:** Try to avoid the after-dinner and before-bedtime window. It doesn't allow for much processing time, can be very disruptive to the bedtime routine, and may create sleep challenges.
   c. **Sweet spot:** Most of my clients find that a Saturday morning affords everyone time to process the divorce news throughout the day and into Sunday, before returning to school or their summer routine.
2. **WHERE will the conversation happen?** Spaces carry energy and hold memories, so be thoughtful about the location.
   a. **Comfort zone:** Often it is a room in the house where everyone can feel comfortable. Remember, the location will be associated with this moment going forward.
   b. **Private:** Some kids do better outside, walking, or on a drive. These are certainly viable options if that is going to be best for your kiddo. Just be sure it's a private location where emotions don't need to be contained or censored.
3. **WHAT will you say?** There are a handful of things every child should hear during this conversation.
   a. **Love:** *We love you, that will never change.*

b. **Care:** *We are your parent team, and we are still going to take care of all the grown-up stuff.*

c. **Unity:** *Our decision to divorce has nothing to do with you. You are the heart of our family, and we will still be a family.*

   i. It's beneficial if you can come to the conversation as a unified team.

   ii. Use the words *us* and *we*. This is a gift to your kids who certainly don't want to be the mediator or referee to their parents' relationship. It also lets them know they don't have to take sides.

d. **Normalcy/continuity:** It's important to remind kids what is *not* going to change: i.e. schools, neighborhood, friend groups, specific family traditions, and so on.

e. **Honesty:** Don't provide false promises. Avoid using the words *maybe* or *possibly*. If you don't have answers to their questions, say so. For example: *We aren't sure where the dog will live, but as soon as we figure that out, you'll be the first to know.*

f. **Create a game plan:** It's helpful to determine who is going to start the conversation and who is going to end the conversation. Everything in between is unknown, depending on your kids' reactions. Have an exit strategy you have thought through and agreed on before you begin the conversation. Maybe you'll head off to an activity, a walk with the dog, or a shared meal. It's also possible that your child will want some time alone—follow their lead.

g. **Nuts and bolts:** Here are a few phrases that might be helpful to get the conversation started for your family:

   i. *We want to talk to you about something important.*

>   **ii.** *You've probably noticed that we've been pretty grumpy/ angry with each other lately. We don't want you to be exposed to that all the time.*
>   **iii.** *You deserve a more peaceful home and joyful parents.*
>   **iv.** *We've been working hard on our relationship but have finally made the really hard decision to get a divorce.*
>
> **h. PAUSE**: Once the word *divorce* has been spoken, let it sit. Don't rush to fill in the gaps and keep talking. Your kids need time to absorb your big news. Leave room for them to have their organic personal reaction. Resist the urge to fill the silence.
>   **i.** *What comes to mind when you think about divorce?*
>   **ii.** *Do we know some families that live in two homes?*
>
>   This is a great way to meet your kids where they are at, without projecting your own divorce beliefs onto them. Ask the following:
>   **i.** What do they understand about it?
>   **ii.** What have they seen with friends?
>   **iii.** What are their fears?
>
>   Take time to listen and respond to what is being said, not just what's spinning around in your head.

4. Allow time/be flexible: The initial conversation might take 10–20 minutes or an hour. Follow your childrens' lead and lean on your intuition to know when it is time to shift gears. Here's an example:

> *This isn't the only time we are going to talk about this change. As you think about things, you might have more questions or big feelings that come up, which is totally normal. We are here for you.*

I also encourage parents to consider the important people in the lives of their kiddos, and how to create safety by informing their circle of support. Teachers, coaches, and school counselors will be better equipped to support your child(ren) if they are provided with the essential information. I'm always astonished how often this is a forgotten detail. If the family dog died over the weekend, or heaven forbid, a family member, we would certainly tell our child's circle of support what happened. In this case, there is a significant death taking place—the death of their family and life as they knew it.

Kids can also get anxious and wonder the following: *Who knows about the divorce? Do I have to tell them? Are they going to ask me questions?* It can be a great relief to your kids if you remove the burden of being the messenger. The following example is what I refer to as the *Family Public Service Announcement*. In Chapter 7, I'll discuss more communication recommendations for your larger community. But here's a simple template you can use to create an announcement you can send to your kids circle of support:

Dear Teachers/Staff/Coaches,

We are writing to share some personal news that affects our family. We have made the difficult decision to separate and will be moving forward with a divorce.

Our highest priority is (child's name)'s well-being and ensuring this transition is as smooth and gentle as possible for them. We are completely united in our commitment to co-parenting them with love and stability. To help us navigate this compassionately, we are working with (The Good Divorce Academy or name of your divorce support team) to ensure we keep our child at the center of every decision we make as a team.

We wanted to make you aware of this change, so we can all partner together to support them. We know that changes at home can sometimes manifest at school/activities, and we would be grateful if

> *you would keep an extra eye on them and let us know if you notice any changes in behavior, mood, or academic engagement.*
>
> *Going forward:*
>
> - *__Communication:__ We ask that you please include both of us on all email communications regarding our child. If there are schedules or important documents to be reviewed, please send two copies home with our child. We will both remain actively involved in their education.*
> - *__Conferences and Events:__ We both plan to attend parent-teacher conferences and school events, sometimes together and sometimes separately, but never with hostility.*
> - *__Logistics:__ We will coordinate the schedule and school logistics between ourselves to ensure there is no disruption for our child(ren).*
>
> *Thank you for the incredible care and support you show (child's name) every day. We deeply appreciate our partnership with you and the entire school/activity community.*
>
> *Sincerely, (sign both parent names)*

SETTING THE STAGE

In theater, there's a clear distinction between what happens onstage and offstage. Onstage you present the performance the audience needs to see. Offstage you might be dealing with forgotten lines, broken props, or personality conflicts. But the audience never sees that. The show must go on, and it must appear unified and seamless.

When we were "onstage" with our children—at school events, during transitions between homes, at birthday parties—we were a parenting team. We smiled at each other, communicated respectfully, and showed our children that Mom and Dad were okay, even if we weren't. Whatever frustrations or conflicts we had were "offstage" matters, dealt with through emails, texts, and phone calls when the kids weren't around and certainly not at a public event.

At the same time, we didn't lie to our kids, but we did omit unnecessary details. If they asked questions about the divorce, we answered honestly but appropriately: "Sometimes, adults realize they work better living in different homes, but we both love you just as much as always." What it meant was never, ever disparaging each other in front of them. No eye rolls when Dad was mentioned. No heavy sighs when Mom's rules were different.

Our "onstage" personas were cooperative co-parents, mature adults who knew how to get along. It's a burden for kids to filter bitter comments about someone they love—because chances are, they love both of you. I wish I could say that I was more successful in this arena. For about three years, the best version of myself was weathered and worn. I wasn't always able to compartmentalize my feelings in the moment, so my emotions showed and things were said. I certainly have regrets. Our kids will find good therapists to help them unravel the imperfections of their parents, and childhood, just like I did.

PROTECTING THEIR FUTURE

When I start working with a new family, we establish a few agreements:

1. Do no more harm.
2. This is not couples counseling.
3. We will not focus on the past.
4. We will be future-focused.
5. I work for your kids.

Yes, the kids are my clients. I work for their future wedding day, because they don't want to have to negotiate which parent gets to come to the rehearsal dinner.

We've all heard these divorce mantras:

- "Don't ever speak poorly about your ex in front of your kids."
- "They are part of each of you. When you criticize their other parent, you are also criticizing your child."
- "They get to love each of you, even if you hate each other."

Most rational parents agree, it would be much better for the mental health of their children, if they didn't weigh the kids down with their own personal garbage. However, some days your co-parent just makes your head spin and you erupt. It's impossible to self-regulate big emotions 100% of the time, and I am certainly not immune. Some days, I can't even regulate the medium-sized emotions.

Anya was around 12 years old, and we were enjoying our after-school hike along the ridge line of the North hills, when she called me out. We were talking about upcoming school projects and the plan for the weekend. It quickly became clear that a trip to the craft store was still needed, the project was now tight on time, and patience were already running thin for both of us.

"I don't know why your dad couldn't have taken care of some of this last weekend?" My annoyance wasn't subtle, as I stomped along the trail. "That really would've helped us all out! Why can't he ...," and she cut me off.

"I don't really need to hear all that stuff. That's between you and dad to work out. I don't want to hear about dad from you, like you know everything."

Bam. Ouch. Wow.

She stopped me dead in my tracks. She wasn't wrong. "Oh Anya, you're right, there is no need for that. I'm so sorry. You know I care for your dad.

He is a great dad. I just don't understand why he can't work something like this into the weekend plan? It's not that hard."

"You're doing it *again*," came Anya's deadpan commentary.

I doubled over laughing at myself, "Oh man, I'm so embarrassed. Sorry. Here's the deal, I am going to get it wrong, again. And when I do, you have permission to call me out, like you just did. Your dad and I are going to get annoyed and irritated with each other. That's natural. But I don't want to expose you to that. Sorry. I will surely screw up again by next week, but I'll keep practicing."

This is when we armed our children with two important phrases to help keep themselves out of the middle: "Sounds like a good question for mom/dad." or "You should have that conversation with mom/dad." They also needed tools to help protect their future.

The other common mistake I have been guilty of is placing my kids in the role of "partner." When parents find themselves reaching for support, they might turn to the most readily available person around, their children. Even before I became a divorce consultant and started seeing this pattern among clients, I noticed the urge and danger of doing it in my own home. Mostly innocent acts of engagement, but I am sure there were times when I overshared or had elevated expectations of my kids.

It might sound something like this in your own home:

"Hey kids, can you help me move the couch, and do you think it looks good against the window?"

"Hey kids, I'm not sure we can go on that ski trip, money is super tight right now because of the divorce and all that crap."

"Hey kids, I just had a huge fight with your dad, and I'm in no mood to go to the park."

All the overt and subtle comments that burden our children with adult problems is unfair and inappropriate. Kids get to be kids, and they should never feel responsible for their parents' emotions, finances, or health (physical or emotional).

THE GOOD GUIDE: THE EMOTIONAL BACKPACK

Following is one of many helpful tools developed by Parent Team, an educational hub for co-parents and divorce professionals. I frequently turn to their resources and curriculum when coaching parents. The concept of the *Emotional Backpack* stems from the work of Brandyn Roark Caires and Jen Schimbeno, co-founders of Parent Team.[1] This is the reminder that our words and actions around our kids really do carry a lot of weight.

Imagine your child has a backpack on, and it's empty.
They are running around, carefree, just being a kid. They are free from adult issues, details, and complexities. Imagine the most unburdened, peaceful moment for your child.

Now imagine adding some sand and small stones to their backpack …
Those are the typical burdens of childhood and of being an adolescent. Challenges with friends, parents, school, navigating puberty, dating, learning new things, managing emotions, exploring identity, belonging, being left out, performance, worries, and so forth.

Now imagine adding some larger rocks to their backpack …
Those are the extra burdens that many kids and teens carry with them, such as breakups, learning differences, anxiety, depression, homelessness, food insecurity, substance, social exclusion, bullying, loss, illness, violence, parental mental health struggles, and many more challenges.

---

[1] Roark-Caires, B. and Schimbeno, J. (2022). *Keeping your kids out of the middle: a co-parents' guide.* Independently Published.

Now imagine adding giant boulders to your child's backpack. Notice the immense weight they are trying to carry….

Those are the burdens children and teens aren't meant to carry, including the adult words, actions, behaviors, and emotions that sometimes spill over onto kids. Things that are far too heavy for them to hold. When parents are overwhelmed, stressed, or in chronic conflict, children can become exposed to experiences they were never designed to absorb or understand.

When we make negative comments about our child's other parent, it's like putting boulders in your child's backpack. You are loading them down with adult burdens to carry through life. Children see themselves as part of each of their parents, and when that part of themself is put down, called names, or never spoken of … it becomes a figurative boulder in their backpack.

Examples of how children feel "caught in the middle" or having to choose sides:
- Badmouthing the other parent
- Keeping secrets from parents
- Having to deliver information from the other parent (i.e. acting as the messenger)
- Being asked for information about the other parent
- Having to listen to adult content/information from one parent about the other household
- Feeling that they have to take care of their parent's emotions
- Sending children to do adult responsibilities: asking for money for school events/extracurriculars/lunch or scheduling time with their parents or pick-up and drop-off times

---

Examples of behaviors between parents that can be harmful for children:

- Blaming
- Judgment of the other
- Forcing children to take sides
- Behaviors that intentionally create division and distance in the family, harm the other parent, or harm the relationship between parent and child

Examples of helpful behaviors for unloading the backpack:

- Keeping your children and their relationship with the other parent in focus. Your child has the right to love you both however they choose—without interference
- Helping them to identify and name their emotions
- Helping them make sense of their feelings
- Validating their emotions and helping them to respect their own feelings and sensations
- Repairing after disagreements with your children
- Leaving adult content and details out of conversations
- Managing all parenting time and financial decisions with the other parent and not your child
- Insulating your child from toxic adult conflict

LOVE PIE

Just a sliver of light from the hallway slides through the almost closed door, casting a warm glow on their pillow-squished faces. I usually sit down in the big green chair in their room as they drift off. Sometimes, it's in this quiet moment before they sleep that they start to chatter about what's on their mind (e.g. school stuff, friend stuff, family stuff, what they want for breakfast, etc.).

Anya spoke first, "Are we going to have new brothers and sisters?" she asked. "Because sometimes when your family has a divorce, you get new brothers and sisters."

I felt my eyes widen in surprise. I wondered where this thought bubbled up from, what had been said on the playground at school? The thought of more kids felt overwhelming and complicated, and something I certainly wasn't anticipating or wishing for. Rather than jump in with an answer, which I certainly didn't have, I flip the question back to her and Dwyer.

"New siblings? Huh," I mused, "What do you think about that idea?"

"Oh, that's exciting," Dwyer said. "Maybe we could get a big brother!"

"Or a little sister!" Anya added.

I was so rattled by their fresh and optimistic perspective. I sat still and quiet and tried to imagine future siblings. I thought our family was complete. Here they were dreaming of more people to bring into their family. They had capacity for more love, and here I was ready to be threatened by it.

In response to my furrowed brow, Anya clarified it, for my sake, "Yeah Mama, like you are always telling us, we can always bake more love pie for all the people." Anya was recalling a story I'd told them often, about an experience I had just before Dwyer was born.

During my last trimester of that pregnancy, I went to one of my mama-mentors in tears. I waddled into Gretta's tearoom early on a Saturday morning and plopped myself down on the lone stool. "It's just, just, everything seems so hard right now," I said, trying to keep it together. "I don't know how I'm going to love this new baby as much as Anya. She already has my whole heart."

Gretta walked over from the counter and set a cup of tea down in front of me, Montana Gold, one of my favorites.

"Thanks," I said quietly, letting the warmth of the handmade mug seep into my heart.

"Karen," Gretta said, sitting down next to me. She sighed as she settled back. She had a mug of tea as well. "Don't worry about loving your second baby. You have so much love to give, we all do."

"But …" I started to protest.

"Think of it like a pie, a love pie. It's very normal to think, as a young mother, that there is only one love pie for your kids. And to think that with each child, it means you will be slicing it into smaller and smaller pieces, leaving the kids with less and less." She wrapped a hand around her own mug and fiddled with the tea bag. "But that's not how it works," she continued on. "When your second child is born, Karen, you don't take a slice of Anya's pie; your son will get a whole new pie—just for him. You will love them both deeply and differently. Don't worry about that. Every child gets their own love pie."

I reassured Anya, "Yes, we will bake more love pie for anyone who joins our family."

IN THEIR OWN WORDS

The Good Divorce Show

Season 1, Episode 3

Kelly and Kyle

Never Married

One Daughter – separated when she was 18 months old

Listen to the full episode here:

TOGETHER APART

Karen: Today, we're chatting with Kelly and Kyle, co-parents, never married, lived together for a hot minute (about 18 months), and then separated. Even though there was not a legal marriage, as soon as you bring children into this life, there is a marriage of DNA, and a forever relationship. You will go on and share graduations, ballet concerts, funerals, and weddings, even grandbabies. Those will be shared experiences for the two of you, through your daughter, Charlotte, who is currently seven.

Early on, you recognized that you were not going to live together, but you would raise a child together. At the time, you made the decision Charlotte was quite young, 18 months old. One of the first decisions that co-parents have to start working with is, how are we going to schedule our child's life? What feels appropriate to their age and to our lifestyle?

How did you navigate those decisions, and how have they changed over the last seven years, if at all?

Kyle: Yeah, it seemed sensible to split the week in half, because you don't have to go too long without seeing your kid, and you also aren't carrying a big load. Especially when she was one and a half, where you're going 10 days in a row, which can also lead to burnout as a solo parent with a toddler.

Karen: What was that journey like for you, Kelly?

Kelly: You know, I mean to be honest, it's so long ago now. I do remember absolutely missing Charlotte, I mean for sure. But I also remember the benefit of having time to recover as a single parent. I knew pretty quickly that I wasn't going to be a full-time mom. I knew I liked having time to myself, and to still be working and being creative. I truly believe that doesn't mean I love Charlotte any less than parents who are there full-time.

I do think Charlotte's a very physical child, so she was extremely attached to me, not just when she was breastfeeding but also just in general. But as far as Charlotte goes, I definitely missed her. I think the hardest part was when she was still so young and so attached to me. Kyle can probably speak to this, but it did feel a bit challenging for her when we had to do the switch.

Karen: Transitions can be really disruptive for kids and parents alike.

Kyle: I think there were times, honestly, the earlier switches when she was like one and a half, there was less cognition on her part of what was going on, so those weren't brutal. But a little bit later, when she was two to three, those were kind of the worst transitions. Those were the times where I was really feeling the pain of us splitting apart, and the guilt when she was super upset for nearly half an hour after mom leaves.

Karen: Did you ever find a hack or a transition method that worked better for all of you? Some parents only transition in and out of school or meet in a park.

Kyle: No, we never did that. That always felt weird to me. It felt better to do it in one of our respective homes, because that was a safe place for her to feel what she needed to feel. If she was going to be upset, I wanted her to be at home and feel safe.

For me, the tactic was just that this was my responsibility to sit with it and to be as patient as I could be. Ultimately, it was my fault, or our fault, for deciding to have a kid after dating for three months and not get married. I felt like I had to pay that debt, however long she was going to be upset after mom leaves.

Karen: I think you make a good point about not wanting to judge. Every situation is unique. You have to follow the lead of your child as much as the lead of your co-parent. At the end of the day, we're all just doing the best we can with the information we have, which means most of us are running around half-blindfolded with scissors in hand, hoping we make it through the day.

Kelly: I think what feels different is that there was no animosity between us. We never had to make a plan about if we could be in the same room together, or not. When I talk to friends who are recently divorced or co-parenting, that's actually the issue. It's less about the child and more about their comfortability as a couple.

Charlotte is a kid. She has strong emotions. We weren't trying to avoid that. We were letting her be upset in a nurturing way. We were all together. Even though we could have made a plan to use a third party, there was something about being in it together.

Kyle: We both had backgrounds in early childhood education. Kelly and I had done preschool teaching. I think we trusted our instincts with a kid that young and what they would need.

Karen: You highlight something so important: the need to feel their feelings. Parents want to whisk it away. Letting the child feel the feelings, and knowing that sadness is temporary, is so important.

Kelly: Charlotte is just a tightly attached child. Dropping off at preschool through first grade, she would hold on and scream bloody murder. She just did not want to separate from us. I don't know if that was specific to our situation or just who she is.

Now, in second grade, she's like, "see ya." She's so adaptable. She settles right in after a few minutes. I genuinely think that's her personality. Nature versus nurture. I think she's going to be a traveler.

Karen: There may be something there.

Kelly: She adapts really quickly. She's a bit of a chameleon. When she's with her dad, parts of her personality come out more. It's really fun to watch.

Kyle: That is fun to watch.

Karen: That would make sense. This is her normal. Charlotte won't have primary memories of one intact household. She has always lived in the abundance of multiple homes and many people loving on her. Divorce often brings a scarcity mindset, but we miss what is happening as a result of two loving families.

Did you ever have a parenting plan?

Kyle: No, we never did. We talked about it when we first separated and then we just didn't. A year went by and we never discussed it again. It was working. We were lucky there were no big clashes. Holidays were never an issue. If Kelly needed coverage, I did it. If I needed coverage, she did it.

Kelly: It's worth mentioning that we're both creative types. We understand each other's worlds. I understand what Kyle goes through when he's about to open a show, and vice versa.

Karen: You're both active in the performing arts, which requires flexibility. And you really cover each other and have each other's backs. It's so great for everyone when that spirit can transcend into a two-household family. Does it also carry over into money? How did you navigate finances?

Kyle: I was really lucky that Kelly figured out a lot of the financial stuff. Insurance, doctor, dentist. We didn't do preschool or paid childcare for the first three years, because of how our schedule worked. It was cost-effective, so there wasn't much to discuss financially.

Kelly: I handled the appointments. Kyle was fine with that. I claim Charlotte on my taxes and get the childcare credit, which covers extracurriculars like gymnastics and ballet. Day-to-day expenses are covered by whoever she's with. It hasn't been an issue yet.

Kyle: If she continues with gymnastics, it'll get expensive. But we have a good groundwork. We cover what we can, and we have family and friends if we need help.

Karen: So, there's never been a battle over a spreadsheet.

Kyle: There were preschool payments where Kelly was like, you're behind. And I was like, sorry, and then I took care of it.

Karen: The lightheartedness you bring to that part of your relationship is so encouraging and inspiring. You are also a unique family because you continue to have movie nights together, with new partners and step kids. You have even shared vacations all together. What prompted you to start that conversation and to follow through with it?

Kyle: I think the first time we shared a trip together was going to Chicago for Kelly's marriage celebration with her new husband, Mike. They were married in Montana, and we basically went to celebrate with her extended family there. So, that was the first one.

Kelly: Kyle's new partner, Melanie, met my whole family on that trip. We just wanted to share all those moments together and let Charlotte have time with both sides of her family.

Kyle: I think we had done enough hanging-out time and movie nights as a whole family at home. That went well. We all enjoyed that. And we knew it would probably be really fun to make a vacation work like that too.

Kelly: Kyle still has family in Lake Forest, Illinois, and that area. So, we both have a connection there. There's a reason for both of us to go to Chicago. We've talked about going to Mexico together. We've talked about going to San Diego together. I think this is kind of the beginning. Getting to Chicago regularly is a really nice ritual.

I like that Charlotte can see her grandparents—on both sides. She met her great grandma in Lake Forest, Kyle's grandmother. And even when Kyle wasn't traveling at the same time as me, I would go see his family in Chicago and bring Charlotte, and make sure she stayed connected to her dad's side of the family. It goes deep.

Kyle: And we know this is rare. Even at Kelly and Mike's wedding ceremony, Mike talked in his vows about how special our shared family is. I stood up during the ceremony … while they said their vows. That sounds like a nightmare on paper, but it was a really special moment for our shared family.

My model for divorce—and I think almost everyone from my generation and before—the model is war and hell. That was such a huge priority, to not model that for Charlotte. And luckily, we're not just pretending our way through it. We do like each other and actually love each other.

Kelly: Right.

Karen: It is rare and amazing. And yet, it's such a simple equation. Choose love. Just choose love and write the story from there.

CHAPTER FIVE

THE HOME

REFLECTION: ONE FOR YOU, ONE FOR ME

Every night after Anya and Dwyer were tucked into bed, we'd sit in the kitchen sorting through the physical artifacts of our shared home. Each object washed in the story of our entangled life.

This process of sorting, negotiating, and deciding was a necessary evil we had to face. We'd been methodically working through drawers and cabinets in the kitchen, dividing dishes, glasses, and cookware with surprising ease. Then we reached the utensil drawer. I pulled it open and began sorting through spatulas, wooden spoons, and measuring cups.

"Which of these do you want?" I asked, holding up a handful of spatulas.

David looked up from the cabinet he was inventorying. "You can keep most of them. I just need a couple for basic cooking."

I nodded and started dropping a collection into the box he started. As the wooden spoon landed, so did reality.

"We were never going to do this one for you, one for me *bullshit!" My anger was eclipsed only by my sadness.*

David sighed. When I looked at him, his eyes were watery, but ever-the-stoic he held back the emotions and didn't move to comfort me. The reality of our separation suddenly overwhelmed me.

Our family would never be whole in the same way, again. There would be no more family dinners with all of us around the same table; no more holidays in one home. We'd be divided, with our children shuttling between two house-holds. All the uncertainty—how we would manage birthdays, vacations, and school events—crashed over me as I stood there in our kitchen, counting spatulas, as if it mattered.

For me, the future I'd imagined was imploding. And there was no one to be angry with. This was a collective effort; we were both culpable in the outcome of our marriage. We had tried so hard, and it still didn't work. What was the point of trying all those years, just to end up here? Maybe we never should've been married in the first place?

"What about the piano?" I asked, through tears.

"You should keep the piano," came David's steady response. "Your dad is the one who found it for us at that auction. Besides, they are a pain in the ass to move, and I'm not going to have room at my place."

"Yeah, that all makes sense," I conceded. "Then you should take the king size bed."

"But you love that bed," he deferred to me.

I resisted, "You also love it, and your dad built that beautiful walnut bed frame. I can't take that. It will become a family heirloom. It needs to be with you."

And so, the process continued as we moved through every room in the house. I kept the larger of the two couches, he took the love seat. I kept the rocking chair that held so many memories of my days nursing the babies. Eventually, this would become the master list David would use on moving day, which happened to land on my 40th birthday. A U-Haul driven by my soon-to-be ex-husband was the last thing I wanted to see on my birthday. We decided the kids and I would be gone for the day.

Despite our differences, there was a gentleness between us. We agreed that it was a shared responsibility to establish two functional homes for our kids. These weren't just decisions about possessions; they were small acts of kindness and acknowledgment of what mattered to each other—a kind of care that seemed both necessary and impossible.

HOME NOT HOME

The physical home holds so much attention and energy for a family during a divorce. It is literally the roof over their heads. It holds all the family traditions and stories. The decisions being made around the home loom like heavy question marks in the divorce process.

I've had clients begin the process, very clear about selling the home, and then pivot two months later when one of them decides to retain the home, and vice versa. This is one of the benefits of *divorce by design* instead of *divorce by default*. The Good Divorce Method follows a progressive mediation process over weeks or months, which allows for more options to surface as couples make giant, consequential decisions, compared to a traditional courtroom battle or day-long marathon mediation process.

The transition from one shared home to two separate homes can be one of the most jarring emotional shifts in early divorce. When one parent stays in the family home and the other moves out, familiar spaces—your kitchen, your garage, your front door—can suddenly feel foreign. One client described standing on the porch of the home they'd lived in for years, unsure whether to knock, ring the bell, or just wait. That hesitation captures the deeper shift from "ours" to "yours," a difficult moment even amicable divorces can't avoid.

One client shared with me his first attempt to host a shared family birthday for their daughter. He'd retained the family home and recounted how strange it was when his ex-wife arrived, walking through the front door like any other guest, even though she had been a resident just a few weeks earlier. They exchanged cordial hellos, "Then she headed straight for the oversized chair in the corner and plopped herself down. And then didn't move."

He continued his rant about how the afternoon unfolded, "As I managed the roast in the crock pot and chatted with relatives, she stayed glued to the chair. While I cleared appetizer plates and set the table, she chatted with my sister. When drinks needed refilling, she still didn't budge." Clearly, he was exasperated by his ex-wife's actions, or in this case, inaction. "The only time she made a move was to get in the photo with our daughter."

I listened empathetically and acknowledged his frustration. Of course, the familiar irritations bubbled up—it was the same person he was married to. However, they were in new territory, redefining household boundaries and expectations. I suggested, "Consider her position for a moment. She was probably feeling uncomfortable and awkward, wondering if she should knock or ring the doorbell, or just come in. Afterall, this was her house just weeks ago and she knew exactly what her role was then. It's possible she didn't know how to help. She didn't know how to be in *her* house, that is now *your* house."

My client's harsh edge softened as he considered the other side of this story. Was she a guest? A co-host? Could she go into the kitchen and start pulling plates from the cabinets? Was she allowed to grab the water pitcher and help refill drinks? "It sounds like she was simply lost," I added.

This couple would have benefited from a pre-event conversation to clarify those roles and household boundaries. The best time to have a conversation about boundaries is before they've been crossed.

BOUNDARIES

Boundaries are the distance at which I can love you and me simultaneously.

— *Prentis Hemphill*

In a co-parenting relationship, boundaries become more than a psychological concept—they become a practical roadmap. Establishing boundaries at the onset of the divorce is not about exclusion; it's about clarity. Clear agreements, such as how and when pickups happen, whether a parent enters the house or waits outside, and what exceptions are allowed, provide structure where emotions may still be tender.

Drs. Henry Cloud and John Townsend have written extensively on the topic of boundaries. "We can't manipulate people into swallowing our boundaries by sugarcoating them. Boundaries are a 'litmus test' for the quality of our relationships."[1] Establishing boundaries is a way of prioritizing

---

[1] Cloud, H. and Townsend, J. (1992). *Boundaries: when to say yes, how to say no to take control of your life.* Zondervan.

your well-being (and emotional health), it's necessary. A simple rule: never drop in on your co-parent's home without sending a flare (i.e. a text or call). Unless you've mutually agreed otherwise, unannounced visits are off limits. Some co-parents prefer an open-door policy, while others pull up the drawbridge and dig a moat. What matters is agreement.

A client once ranted, "I don't care if he waltzes into my house, I'm not all wound up about it. He won't even let me in the front door! What gives?"

My response was, "Having the same boundaries is not a requirement. Respecting each other's boundaries is." I struggled with this myself early on, missing my kids so much that I sometimes overlooked my co-parent's limits. Healthy boundaries make for healthy relationships, before and after divorce.

SECOND HOME

Before David officially moved, we agreed it would help settle the kids' anxiety and curiosity to go see his new home. By which I mean, I needed to go see his new home to settle my anxiety and curiosity. Just short of begging, I asked if I could be a part of that first field trip. I needed to see where my little babies would be when they weren't with me. Not because I didn't trust David, or thought it might not be a suitable place. I just needed to have the image in my mind to feel close to them, even when apart. I couldn't imagine being able to sleep if I didn't know where they were sleeping, where the other half of their life was happening.

They burst through the door with excitement. "There's a fireplace," exclaimed Dwyer. Anya followed suit, "Look at how big our room is." My tender heart felt a stab over their excitement. Logically, it was great that they were excited. That was an ideal response. Emotionally, everything felt like a loss to me. Where they saw abundance, I saw scarcity.

After the field trip, the kids rode home with me in the minivan. I drove without speaking, trying to make sense of what felt totally surreal. Dwyer broke the silence, "Mama, I should probably have *two* bottles of vitamins and *two* toothbrushes," he said from his car seat. "One for both of my bathrooms."

I was momentarily surprised. While I was worrying about how sad or scared or confused my kids might be, it seemed they were already embracing the new reality. I was the one currently wrapped with worry and grief. We made sure there was a vitamin bottle at each home. Dwyer and Anya each picked out new toothbrushes. We found that duplicating as much as possible made everyone's life easier. When the kids were younger, it was easy to have a set of books, toys, and clothes in both locations. As they grew older, they became more particular about their stuff and wanted more items to transition with them between homes (e.g. skateboards, makeup, jewelry, favorite high-tops). Together, we were learning how to be one family living across two homes.

NEW HOME

It had been almost two years since we became a 2Home Family. I finally sold the family home and moved to a new house on Tulip Court. I hadn't fully appreciated the negative weight of staying in our marital home until I left it. I wouldn't have done anything differently at the time. It was a gift to provide that familiar and stable environment for the kids, while so much else was changing around them. But boy howdy, I was so happy to move into a new home and truly start fresh.

David had settled into a long-term property as well, just six blocks down the street from me. With the kids' elementary school stationed between us, this became our family's Bermuda Triangle for 12 years. From kindergarten to college, we were able to give our kids a shared neighborhood and homes they could safely walk and bike between. Close proximity isn't always possible. But if it is, I highly recommend it. A *2Home* life is complicated; there's a lot of gear schlepping and chasing down forgotten items. Our close proximity definitely contributed to the success of our divorce.

One of our most impactful linguistic choices we made was how we would speak about our family homes. Instead of referring to our homes as "Mom's House" and "Dad's House," which felt possessive and divisive, David and I intentionally referred to our homes by their street names: *Tulip* and *Robert*. This was a deliberate strategy to help our children feel equal ownership and fully at home in both places.

By removing parental ownership from the home names, we deemphasized the separation between David and me, while emphasizing the children belonging in both spaces. They weren't shuttling between Mom's territory and Dad's territory, like small ambassadors negotiating between warring nations; they were living life across *their* two homes.

2HOME FAMILY

The language used to describe divorced families sets a tone and expectation throughout society. We chose to adopt language that better reflects how we saw ourselves, *"We are one family that lives across two homes,"* also called a 2Home Family. I didn't like saying the word *divorce* and enduring all the implications that come with it. Divorce implies a distinct division and invites people to choose sides. The restructuring of our family wasn't about going to battle; David and I weren't opposing forces. By using the terminology of *one family, two homes*, I hoped others understood we were still working together to raise our kids—it just looked different now.

When it came to guiding our children through the divorce-*ing*, David and I tried to strike the balance between doing *to* and doing *with*. We made sure Anya and Dwyer were included but were not responsible for the transition to living across two homes. They were able to pick the books and toys they wanted to take to the new house. Our furniture was divided between houses to maintain consistency, and it financially made sense. The kids would see familiar pictures, plants, furniture, utensils, and plates. We wanted both spaces to feel comforting and homey to the kids.

We stumbled into the idea of hanging photos of each other in our respective homes. Yes, I have lived with photos of my co-parent in my home, not next to my bed or on the fridge, but next to the kids' beds and in their play spaces. David also created a collage of photos of me with the kids to hang in their bedroom at his home. When they were young, this allowed the kids to feel close to both of us, even when we were apart. Worth noting, if my first husband had actually died, we would very likely have photos of him in the house, and no one would think twice about it.

We took turns shopping with the kids to pick up items we knew had to be duplicated, and we split all the costs 50/50. It seemed unfair for the spouse moving out to carry the burden of all the moving expenses. We saw it as a shared responsibility to establish two functional homes for the kids. David and I kept our shared bank account until all of the moving expenses had been paid.

It took about three years for both of us to finally settle into what would become our family homes for the next 12 years. During that time, I began to find some financial stability, the cadence of the schedule began to normalize, and I discovered how to embrace my new part-time mama-life, built for one.

TRANSITIONS

Living part-time in a home can be disruptive and exhausting, especially for the kids who might feel like traveling salesmen living out of a suitcase. It is likely that you and your co-parent manage your homes differently, and your kids have to adapt every time they transition. Small changes in the bedtime routine, food choices, and expectations around chores and homework all require kids to adapt and be flexible. Arguably, they're all good skills to have in life, but their impact on children shouldn't be underestimated.

Co-parenting specialist Christina McGhee, MSW, reminds us, "Children tend to function best when they know what to expect. For many, moving between Mom's house and Dad's house literally feels like transitioning between two worlds. When children don't have an opportunity to regroup, often their anxiety levels go through the roof."[2] She encourages parents to pay attention to changes in mood and behavior and to watch for patterns. Does a transition that takes place in a neutral environment tend to go more smoothly than directly from house-to-house? Perhaps your kiddo needs private time in their room when they arrive. Are they tired or hangry as they go into a transition? Look for the clues, your children are communicating their needs to you, even if they can't articulate it explicitly.

Not only are the kids constantly adjusting, so are the parents. I anticipated a significant adjustment as soon as they walked out the door with their dad. What I didn't expect was the significant adjustment when they returned. Simply put, transition days were disruptive for all of us, and it didn't change with age. It would always take about 24 hours to settle in with each other and our shared routines. For this reason, as kids age, it can be helpful to extend the time in each house, reducing the number of transitions per month. This allows everyone to coalesce in that home environment and find their groove.

What worked for our children at ages five and six evolved as they aged. We switched to a week-on-week-off schedule once Patrick started second grade. As they entered middle school, they let us know the constant back-and-forth felt disruptive. They wanted more time to settle into each household, less schlepping their belongings around for activities, and fewer transitions.

Coming out of the pandemic, after being settled for long periods of time at both homes, they came to us and requested a two-week rotation. David and I agreed we could make that work. When Anya left for college, Dwyer became

---

[2] McGhee, Christina. (2024). Get back to calm and carry on: helping kids transition between each parent's household—divorce and children. *Divorce and Children—Helping Separated and Divorced Parents Raise Happy and Secure Kids* (blog) (accessed December 5, 2024). https://divorceandchildren.com/helping-kids-transition-between-households-after-divorce/.

a solo nomad and requested a month-to-month schedule. His comment to us, "If I knew I was going to be in one place for a month, then it would be worth packing up my computer system, moving it, and setting it up again. It would be cool to have my set up with me wherever I'm at." We agreed.

This is a good example of the kids' voices informing a parental vote. It might be hard to imagine an entire month away from your kids. I certainly couldn't have fathomed such a reality early in our divorce. However, once the kids had access to a car, they wanted to live more like free-range chickens between their homes, outside the rigidity of a residential schedule dictated by us, or worse yet, a court. There were plenty of extracurricular activities, celebrations, and opportunities to be with the kids. But like most teenagers, the schedule was no longer about us.

In the early years, when the kids transitioned, it was common for me to sweep through the house in a cleaning frenzy. For me, mindless cleaning is incredibly therapeutic, and a clean house brings a steady calm to my otherwise anxious self. The fort made from blankets and pillows under the dining table—dismantled. The giant Lego contraption blocking the stairway—returned to the plastic bin for storage. The half-completed puzzle covering the bedroom floor—literally swept up. These were rare and remarkable moments when my entire house would be clean all at once and stay that way.

Then, my little roommates would return. I was so excited to have the kids back home. However, within moments of landing, they would start moving things around, dropping piles of kid detritus everywhere, and leaving dirty dishes in their wake. I also had to start cooking again. My pendulum would swing wildly from single-woman life to single-parent life, and it was a stark contrast. I would like to say that I was able to move through my irritability quickly and without notice, but that wasn't always the case.

Then, the questions would start. "Mama, why did you break my Lego sculpture?" "I was almost done with that puzzle, now I have to start all over again." "Where is our fort?" I came to realize my impulse for an orderly home was essentially erasing my kids from their home, and they felt it. Eventually, I came to think of their exit as a pause button on the remote. To the best of my ability, I would leave their projects, essentially their fingerprints, untouched while they were gone. Psychologically, I could see this helped with transitions; it was easier to push play and pick up from where we left off when they returned.

ROOMMATES NO MORE

If David and I had met through a roommate-wanted ad online, we probably would've passed. But marriage, sure, why not? I laugh about it now. A contributing factor to the unraveling of our marriage, in my opinion, was the fact that we were terrible roommates. It became a gnawing issue and point of conflict. Recently a podcast host asked me if I had a theory as to why 70% of divorces are initiated by women.[3] I can't speak for all women but for me, deep resentment stemming from the unequal distribution of domestic and emotional labor certainly took a toll on our marriage.

Balancing household and emotional labor isn't just about fairness—it's essential for the health of a relationship. Over time, this imbalance can erode connection and respect, leaving women feeling unseen, exhausted, and undervalued in their own homes. As Eve Rodsky writes in her book, *Fair Play*, "When both partners feel seen and valued for what they contribute, the relationship shifts from resentment to respect, from exhaustion to partnership. By sharing responsibility fully and equitably, couples can transform daily life from a source of tension into a foundation for love."[4] Well, we missed that boat.

---

[3] Rosenfeld, David J. (2014). Who wants to break up? Gender and the dissolution of heterosexual relationships. *American sociological review* 79(6), 1133–1158.

[4] Rodsky, Eve. (2019). *Fair play: a game-changing solution for when you have too much to do (and more life to live)*. G.P. Putnam's Sons.

Ironically, through divorce and our agreement to be 50/50 parents, I finally had the balanced parenting partnership I said I wanted. I felt like I had more energy and focus for my children as they grew up. I would never pursue divorce for the purpose of a more egalitarian domestic life, but it's a nice benefit. Perhaps if more couples addressed this imbalance while living together, it would improve marital satisfaction and outcomes. We tried.

In our new reality, David could let dishes pile up at his house without the presence of a nagging wife. When he forgot to wipe down the counter or left dirty socks lying around, it was no longer my problem. He was at his place and I was at mine, and we could create our own comfortable habitats. The feeling of freedom didn't come right away; I have controlling tendencies and letting go doesn't come easily, especially when it comes to my children. Fortunately, I have always trusted him as a father, and how he keeps his space is no longer my concern. Slowly, I began to relax as the weight of managing my own household alone got easier, and I cared less and less about what was happening at David's. We started to find our 2Home groove. And I could load the dishwasher just the way I wanted.

THE GOOD GUIDE: SUCCESSFUL TRANSITIONS

1. Coordinate meetups.

- When possible, coordinate transitions with your kids' school pickups or after an activity. This can ease the transition for kids. Sometimes, leaving the current home can highlight departure and might bring bigger feelings.
- Avoid public confrontations—neutral transition locations are best, if tension exists.
- Don't turn transitions into parent meetings. It's not the time to *get into it*.

2. **Stick to the schedule.**
   - Stick to a predictable schedule, so children know what to expect.
   - Allow extra time during transitions to avoid rushing or last-minute stress.
   - Communicate any changes well in advance.
   - Honor the set schedule and time of your co-parent.

3. **Preserve your kids' space.**
   - Keep their belongings in their usual places.
   - Maintain familiar routines, rooms, and comfort items.
   - Avoid removing special projects they may have started but not yet finished.

4. **Let their story unfold.**
   - Resist interrogating children about the other parent's household.
   - Ask gentle, open-ended questions without the expectation that you will get a satisfactory answer.
   - Do not ask children to relay messages or updates between the two of you.
   - Avoid involving them in adult conflicts or negotiations.
   - Protect them from adult responsibilities and stress.

5. **Create transition traditions.**
   - Have a transition tradition, such as a puzzle or craft project waiting, or taking the dog on a walk. This can provide a supportive bridge as they arrive.
   - Give your kids space to transition emotionally without pressure. It's often a significant adjustment to move between homes.
   - Validate your kids' feelings: listen without judgment to fears, excitement, or sadness.

6. **Learn the logistics.**
    - Pack clothing, schoolwork, and any gear for activities the night before a transition. At the very least, remind your kids there is a transition day coming up.
    - Things will be forgotten. Be patient with your kids; they didn't choose to live across two homes.
    - When possible, try to live near each other, as close proximity will be a benefit to everyone.
    - Be supportive of your co-parent when things are forgotten. Your extra effort is in support of your child's success.
    - You are responsible for getting necessary transition objects to the other home. Do not send your child to school with a suitcase (yes, it has happened).
7. **Create a boomerang folder.**
    - Maintain a folder with items that need to go back and forth between homes (e.g. forms, school notes, artwork, graded homework, etc.).
    - Encourage children to manage the folder with guidance, not responsibility.
    - Check and update the folder's contents at each transition, to avoid lost items.
    - Consider using a shared notebook or electronic Google document to keep each other informed about your child's needs, changes, concerns, and celebrations.
8. **Share calendars.**
    - Use a shared calendar (physical or digital) for school events, extracurriculars, and visitation.
    - Use apps like My Family Wizard to communicate schedules, messages, and documents, without involving children.

- Keep children informed by posting a simple calendar in the home. Color coding the calendar can provide an easy visual for kids.
- Ensure both parents update the calendar consistently to avoid confusion.
- Keep your updates professional and focused on logistics.
- Reduce the chance of conflict and miscommunication by centralizing the information.

IN THEIR OWN WORDS

The Good Divorce Show

Season 1, Episode 22

Maggie-Mom and Kara-Daughter

Sisters were 6 and 9 at time of the divorce

Recorded 40 years postdivorce

Listen to the full episode here:

LEAVE FOR THE KIDS

Karen: Did you and your sister have any sort of idea or hint? I think sometimes we have this belief that our kids don't hear and see as much as they do.

Kara: We definitely witnessed them not getting along, struggling to communicate. Arguing—I wouldn't say it was ever too crazy—but I just remember there was tension. There was tension and frustration and something going on.

Karen: Did it ever occur to you that your parents might get divorced?

Kara: I don't think I really thought along those lines. It occurred to me more after, once they told us. I was like, "Okay, that actually makes sense," based on what I'd been seeing and hearing. That's how it came about for me.

Karen: That's a great reminder to our listeners that, as parents, we try to protect our children, but they know. And if they don't actually know, they start making things up. Our imaginations and stories can get really wild. There can be relief and comfort in, "Oh, here's the truth of it." Maggie, would you agree that Kara's sense of tension in the house was accurate in your experience as well?

Maggie: Extremely. The tension was there. I think my age had a lot to do with it. I didn't know how to communicate well, and I take a lot of the blame for that. He was older and could speak his mind, and I wasn't able to do it.

Karen: It's gracious of you to take ownership, even decades later. Without sharing private parts of your life, can you talk about what was going on for you leading up to the decision to leave the marriage?

Maggie: I was a stay-at-home mom for the most part. I felt like there was nothing there for me, except my two children, who I adore. He traveled. I never felt he was there for me, and sometimes not for the girls.

Karen: How old were you and your sister, when you heard about the divorce?

Kara: Nine. Corey was somewhere around six.

Karen: So, elementary school age. Maggie, do you recall your fears and hesitations around making this decision?

Maggie: Nobody ever wants to break up a family. Stability for children that age is so important. But it was to the point where it was making my daughters unhappy. That was probably one of my prime reasons—I didn't want my children to be unhappy.

Karen: We hear "stay for the children," but sometimes, "I need to leave for the children."

Maggie: I had to leave to be a better mother. I was falling into depression. You can't be a good mother when you're like that.

Karen: Do you have memories of that, Kara? Or looking back now, do you see the shift pre- and postdivorce?

Kara: Definitely. I don't think, until I was much older, I could peel back the layers, but at the time it was seeing someone happy who previously wasn't. When I saw my parents move into a place of happiness, it started to click.

Karen: Was having more happy adults in your life beneficial?

Kara: Oh yeah. Looking back, in some ways we became a better family. A stronger family, a healthier family. They treated each other better once they decided to get divorced.

Karen: And you agree, Maggie?

Maggie: Absolutely.

Karen: Do you have a theory on why that happened?

Maggie: Because I was so unhappy, I was making everybody unhappy. Once I got out, I could communicate better. We had to talk about the kids and finances. I didn't communicate well before.

Karen: When it became clear the marriage would dissolve, there's the dreaded conversation: how do we tell the children? Maggie, how did that unfold?

Maggie: It was my first big divorce mistake. I told the girls without him. He was angry—we were supposed to do it together. We didn't really have a plan. We were in the car driving, and it just came out.

Karen: What do you remember from that moment, Kara?

Kara: It's visceral. I remember being in the car. I can picture the area outside of Chicago. It hit me hard—not sadness exactly, just, "Okay, this is strange." I hadn't pictured what this would look like.

Karen: Even decades later, that moment is remembered. Parents are writing a story. The words you use, the location—that becomes something your children carry forever.

After the divorce, you had to go out and get a job Maggie. In your generation, it was common for women to feel held hostage by their marriages, because many didn't have a career. What did you end up doing? What was your professional journey postdivorce?

Maggie: I don't know if it counts or how professional it was, but I was an administrator in a real estate office.

Karen: It all counts, Maggie. It all counts when you go out there to support your children and yourself. It's very impressive. It's a big courageous leap to take that on.

Maggie: I enjoyed it so much, and a little flexibility was involved, which I needed as a single parent. If I had to take off and get one of the girls to a doctor's appointment or something, they were very helpful with that. It really was a gift at that time.

Karen: And not only did you go searching for a job, and a career, and a way to support you and your daughters, but you also decided to go searching for love again or maybe love found you. I would like to hear from both of you a bit about how this new person emerged in the family, and the role he played for all of you.

Maggie: He was actually a friend first. I had another part-time job in a video store, and he had a pizzeria up front. And when he learned about the divorce, you know, well, he had an old table he gave to me, he helped move that in and helped me a lot. Even brought us a Christmas tree that first year—the rest was history!

Karen: And is this man still in the picture?

Maggie: Yes, we've been married for 38 years in September!

Karen: And what do you remember of Rob showing up early on the scene, Kara?

Kara: He was a pretty fun guy. I remember he liked to play the drums; he was really into classic rock. I thought to myself, this guy's pretty cool. He took me to lots of concerts. He and my mom were happy. It wasn't really until I saw my mom happy with another person, that it sunk in for me like, oh wow, okay, this is a good thing; this is better; this feels better. I might not have fully understood why divorce was better at that time, but I could see it was better for her, and it felt better for my sister and I too.

Karen: Oh, that's such a beautiful sentiment and such a beautiful gift that you're offering up to our listeners: for those who are wondering, divorce is only going to damage my children. That is a myth; it is not a truth. And Maggie, did you feel hesitation or excitement as you thought about repartnering?

Maggie: Actually, I was scared. I mean, I kept questioning: am I going to feel this way in 10 years? Am I going to have to go through this again? I was very hesitant and I was very scared. But he was—he is a really good man. I'm very spoiled. So, at any rate, no; it was lovely in the end. Absolutely lovely. And we learned if you try to ignore things, which I did in my first marriage because I didn't want to upset anybody, you're in trouble. Now, if we have something going on, we hit it right on. That is the biggest change for me because that was my biggest failure in my first marriage. I was a bad communicator.

Karen: Sounds like there was more capacity, emotional safety, trust, and you brought a new version of yourself to your second marriage.

Maggie: Well, I was also 11 years older.

Karen: It's amazing what the wisdom of time will do for all of us. And so around age 12, there's this new father figure in your life, Kara. I'm curious how that impacted your relationship with your biological father and still having weekend and vacation time visits with him. You and your sister were heading into the tween years as stepdad, Rob, was showing up. How did it go?

Kara: You know, this is one of the things that I have so much respect for towards my parents. I definitely learned later, once I was older and we could kind of get to the nitty-gritty a little bit more, about emotions and frustrations and feelings they had to work through in those early years after the divorce.

But my dad showed nothing but respect for Rob. He would say all the time that he seemed like a really great guy. And from what he knew of him, he was, and that he was really good for my mom. My dad was awesome about it. It just made it feel really good for me and my sister. And, you know, he might have had some things that he was working through, but at that time and at our ages, he didn't pull us into that. That was his stuff, not our stuff.

I have a lot of respect for that. And it's not because I think we should be dishonest or hide the truth. But now that I am a parent, I know that there are just some things that are mine, that are weights that my kids don't necessarily need to carry.

CHAPTER SIX

THE GRIEF

REFLECTION: PHANTOM PAIN

The fragile leaves of the October evening hung tight to their limbs, hoping it wouldn't be their night to fall. The leaves beneath my feet sculpted a multi-color, golden path. The forest floor smelled like death, decay, and endings. And yet, still beautiful. It was the perfect backdrop to a marriage that was also in decay. And yet, still a beautiful family.

About 20 minutes into my walk through Greenough Park, I rounded a bend and stumbled into a family of four on the wooden footbridge, with a floppy happy dog in tow. Their son, around Dwyer's age, was collecting amber leaves out of a pokey bush, stuffing as many as possible into a bouquet held with one chubby hand. Their tween daughter stood, hands in her jacket pockets, leaning over the bridge's grey weathered railing, watching the golden parade of fall detritus dive and spin down Rattlesnake Creek.

"Look, there's a tree chopper!" the boy exclaimed, pointing into the trees, and all the heads turned.

"Oh yeah, that's a Pileated Woodpecker" came a proud fatherly voice, "Good eye!"

The mother caught the girl's attention and said something that made her crack a reluctant smile and roll her eyes. Mom gave her a playful nudge with an elbow. They appeared to be so easy and happy together. They were complete. I was looking into a false mirror of my future—a future that wouldn't be realized.

I crossed the bridge, going by the family as the boy handed the golden bouquet to his mom, my eyes welling up with tears. I ducked down a hidden trail and headed for the creek bank, the moving water camouflaging my sounds of grief. Had I—had we—made the right decision with this divorce? Would we get to have moments like that family on the bridge? Or did we have to give up everything?

The moving water blurred as my mind spiraled. My body was engulfed with emotion, foremost that of grief, not just for what I'd lost, but for what would never be. I've heard phantom pain described as a sensation of pain at the source of a limb that has been amputated. Seeing the intact family on the bridge was a painful reminder of my absent family. I could feel their presence and absence all at once.

THE SOUNDS OF SILENCE

The house was too quiet when I pushed open the front door. It was 5:30 p.m. on a Sunday in late October 2011, just a week after David had moved out, and I'd just dropped Anya and Dwyer off for their first overnight at their new home. My hands moved on autopilot—keys dropped into the wood bowl, purse placed on the bench, my jacket hung on the hook. I had never experienced such deafening silence. It startled me.

The familiar evening routine kicked in, and I headed straight for the kitchen. I pulled open the refrigerator, scanning the contents, which were pathetic as usual. The kitchen has never been my happy place. My cooking skills seemed to have topped out in my college years, Top Ramen, nachos, toast, mac and cheese, spaghetti, and eggs. It seemed impossible to muster the motivation to cook for myself, but eating out wasn't currently in the budget. I had already started down the path of the *divorce diet*, shedding pounds in the absence of nourishment.

I grabbed a package of Top Ramen, a block of cheese, a couple of eggs, the remnants of a dying onion, and a handful of mushrooms. I welcomed the tearful effects of dicing the onion, which provided permission to open the floodgates again. How can one body produce so many tears? The silence in the house grew louder. I grabbed the CD player and desperately pushed play, caring little about what would come through the speaker. Anything would be a welcome distraction. U2's *Joshua Tree* played. Bono's voice rang true as he sang the iconic, and ironic song "I Still Haven't Found What I'm Looking For." I cranked the volume and let my voice fill the house, half singing, half wailing.

While the food sat warm on the stove, I opened the cupboard, preparing to set the table. What was the point? There was no one there to set a table for. I reached for a bowl and stopped myself. Why bother? It would mean one more lonely dish to clean.

Anya and Dwyer were likely sitting down to dinner with their dad. The realization crashed over me, and my throat tightened. I tried to quell the rising emotion to no avail. I stood alone, crying again, eating directly out of the pan as I hovered over the kitchen counter. It was a scene that would continue to repeat itself for years to come.

The following evening was mildly better, mostly because I knew what was coming, so I left my home office at the end of the day and got the hell out of the house. I would need to ask for support and help, which felt insurmountable. But I knew too much isolation would destroy my mental health. I called friends down the street and asked if I could just come over and hang out with their family. I didn't need anything specific; I just needed to get out of my house and out of my head.

"Yes, of course, come on over," came my girlfriend's calm and welcoming tone. "Do you want to take a relaxing bath when you arrive?"

This couple built a stunning home, and their bedroom suite had a luxurious soaking tub and steam shower. It isn't common practice for neighbors to soak in each other's bathtubs, but this wasn't a common situation. However, this ritual did become common practice for me. For weeks, they indulged my presence in their home, and while I soaked, they went about their usual business downstairs, until they told me it was time to go home and go to bed.

The next day I would have a brighter start, knowing Dwyer and Anya would transition back to my world later that afternoon. These were the early days in our separation and the kids were young, so we had very short rotations between homes, typically two or three nights. I walked over to the elementary school and scooped up Anya, who was full of stories. I was hanging on every word, trying to fill in the gaps from the lost moments of the past two days. We found Dwyer on the playground with his class. I was elated to see them, as if they had been gone for many moons, not many hours. I'm sure I asked far too many questions about the previous 48 hours, which is a habit I learned to break over time. Kids don't want to be met by Barbara Walters when they return home.

When David picked them up two nights later, Dwyer was chatting excitedly about using his Spiderman toothbrush at his new house and sleeping in the bunk beds. I encouraged the enthusiasm outwardly, but internally I was deeply jealous and saddened. I didn't want to let them go. The prospect of two more nights alone hung forebodingly over me.

"Bye, Mama!" Dwyer called, already buckled into his car seat, waving enthusiastically. Anya gave me a longing look through the car window, her six-year-old intuition perhaps picking up on my forced smiles. By 5:15 p.m., they were gone, and the house fell silent again.

I tried to be productive. There were work emails to answer, a project deadline looming, and bills to pay. But I found myself wandering from room to room like a ghost, straightening pillows that were already straight, picking up toys that didn't need picking up. I stood in their bedroom doorway, Anya's American Girl doll propped against her pillow and Dwyer's favorite yellow truck parked under the bed. There they would stay, untouched, as if someone had paused my mama movie.

CAN I GET A CASSEROLE OVER HERE?

In the darkest of moments, a thought crept in: it would be easier if I was widowed. Not because I've ever wished death upon David, but rather because people know how to support a widow. A meal train gets set up immediately.

A rotation of friends checks in every day. An invitation to dinner for all the holidays would come my way for the first year. If I were a widow instead of a divorcée, there'd be support groups and networks of people to talk to. There would be the funeral ritual to help me, the kids, and our extended family process this significant change. My community would process the grief and the change alongside me. There would be a prescribed period of mourning that everyone understood and honored. That would have been swell.

But as a divorcée, no one ever delivered a casserole to my front door. I am not calling out my amazing circle of friends; they did so much for me. Rather, I am making the point that we are missing a blueprint on how best to support families going through divorce.

Let me be clear. I have never wished David dead for one moment of my life. My message isn't for people to choose homicide over divorce. Divorce is still the way to go in that toss-up. But clearly society is underestimating what families of divorce are going through and may not appreciate the grief process that comes with it. My husband didn't die, thank God. But my marriage did, in addition to my identity as a wife and partner. Social structures and friendships might die. Our intact family structure died. And most heartbreaking of all the deaths, my role as a full-time mama died.

Grief over the death of a loved one makes logical sense. Death is final, irreversible, and rarely does someone choose it. Divorce is a different kind of ending. Instead of a physical person ceasing to exist, in divorce you lose abstract concepts like being together as a family unit, imagined future plans, and your identity as a married person. And your former spouse walks around town, very much alive.

American society doesn't know what to do with divorce grief. Divorce is so often depicted as contentious, we forget there is also loss. The anger found between divorcing couples can mask a deep disappointment that our needs haven't been seen or met by our partner. Our love story didn't turn out how we wanted it to. Movies and TV often parody "break-up" grief, depicting women eating pints of ice cream and crying to their friends, and men more or less ignoring whatever feelings they might have. The grief is real, however, and deserves the same respect we give to other forms of loss.

THE DEATH OF A RELATIONSHIP

When a marriage ends there is loss, and divorce is best categorized as an *ambiguous loss*. According to Pauline Boss, the researcher who coined the term, ambiguous loss is categorized by an inability to find closure and understanding.[1] In ambiguous losses, there is still someone living, but they have become unknown to us. The family members of dementia or Alzheimer patients know this loss well. The loved one is still living, but the person you once knew no longer shows up at the table.

Ambiguous loss is also applied to scenarios where a loved one has gone missing (such as a soldier missing in action, or an explorer's body never recovered from a backcountry accident), because the person is gone, yet there is still a chance they might return. Unlike death, which offers finality, ambiguous loss leaves you in limbo without closure. Ambiguous loss can come with life events like a miscarriage, life-altering diagnoses, reckoning with traumatic events, and, of course, the end of a relationship.

The family on the bridge in Greenough Park was living out my future fantasy. I tried to convince myself that David and I could hang out with Anya and Dwyer like that, together in the park. But at the time, only several weeks after starting the divorce process, I was so overwhelmed with grief that no part of me could envision any future with peace and ease.

---

[1] Boss, P. (1999). *Ambiguous loss: learning to live with unresolved grief.* https://archive.org/details/ambiguouslosslea00boss.

THE STAGES

In my work with divorcing couples, I see a predictable pattern in the five *stages of divorce*:

1. Thinking about divorce
2. Deciding to divorce
3. Going through divorce
4. Recovering from divorce
5. Divorce, what divorce?

Most people get stuck in stage three and begin to wonder if there will ever be an end to their suffering. It's at that point I often reference the children's book, *Going on a Bear Hunt* by David Rosen. In this book, a family sets out on an adventure and encounters a series of obstacles—long wavy grass, a deep cold river, thick oozy mud, a dark forest, a swirling snowstorm, and finally the narrow, gloomy cave. Each time they reach a challenge, they repeat the refrain: *"We can't go over it. We can't go under it. Oh no! We've got to go through it!"*

Divorce recovery is no different than this simple story; the only way to get through the grief is to *go through* the grief. Knowing there is life beyond the dark days brings hope and can reduce anxiety. This, in turn, helps everyone bring a little more patience and compassion to the process. At the end of each episode of my podcast *The Good Divorce Show*, I remind listeners, "Everything will be okay in the end. And if it's not okay, it's not the end."

The future possibilities are sometimes forgotten about in the grief process, as we are consumed with the big changes happening in the present. But it's important to name them. If we disregard them or pretend we don't have these future dreams, they'll haunt us. They'll pop up in unexpected moments. When I'm operating from a heart place rather than an angry one, what I am really grieving is the dream that did not come true.

Being re-singled by divorce, I was grieving the change in my identity, from who I was while married, to who I was alone. For eight years, I'd been part of a "we." I often weighed my decisions through the lens of "us." What would I eat if I didn't have to consider someone else's preferences? How would I spend my evenings and weekends? These questions, while seemingly simple, felt overwhelming. I'd spent years compromising and adapting to a world of coupled decision-making.

Of course, when the kids were around, I could still focus on their needs instead of my own. Yet half of the time, it was just me. And for me, the death of being a full-time parent was particularly difficult in the early years. When the kids weren't living with me, my identity vacillated, as I was overwhelmed with the freedom to decide. The kids had become the center point of my decisions and identity. The pendulum swung hard when they were born and now it was swinging back, unexpectedly. It wasn't returning to the previous stasis but into unknown territory. I went through the grief and loss of who I had been *before* their arrival. Now, like an archaeologist, I had to excavate myself out of the rubble of our family.

Over time I would come to appreciate and even embrace my personal freedom, but that wasn't my starting point. All I could think about was how I wouldn't see my kids every morning, padding into the kitchen with their adorable bedheads. I'd miss half the laughing episodes of them playing in the living room while I cooked dinner. I'd be excluded from half the park outings. I secretly hoped the big milestones would happen when the kids were staying with me. In my head, it was an all or nothing, zero-sum equation.

DIVORCE GUILT

Looking back, some of my grief was actually *divorce guilt*. I was failing as a mother because I wouldn't be giving my kids all of me, all of the time. I had terrible repeating mantras in my head:

> *If I wasn't with them, then I should retreat to the prison of my home.*

It would be in poor taste to go have fun during my
"off duty time."
Real parents don't take time off every other week.
No fun for me; I must pay my penance for
thrusting our family into this story.

Society consistently downplays *relationship grief*, particularly for adults. It sometimes seems that because divorce is a "choice," we shouldn't be sad about it—surely, if we're sad about it, we should've stayed together. But as anyone who has been through a significant breakup knows, relationship endings can be necessary and heartbreaking all in the same breath. Attachment bonds form in long-term partnerships (even unhealthy ones), and there's genuine neurobiological pain that occurs when we sever those attachments. When we say, "love hurts," it's real.

THE COMINGS AND GOINGS OF GRIEF

For months after David moved out, I stayed in motion to avoid processing my grief and loneliness. Previously, I used to hate traveling for work and missing time with the kids. But suddenly, when the kids were gone, I threw myself into work trips with newfound enthusiasm, grateful for hotel rooms in distant cities where my loneliness felt temporary and necessary. When I wasn't traveling for work, I visited out-of-town friends, sleeping on couches and in guest rooms—anywhere but the all-too-quiet walls of my own home. I hadn't yet mastered the art of being alone and not lonely.

Divorce grief, like the grief from a deceased loved one, ebbs and flows. The five stages of grief, as outlined by Elizabeth Kubler-Ross (i.e. denial, anger, bargaining, depression, and acceptance), are helpful for understanding what we might be feeling while grieving. However, we don't move through the five stages in a linear path and get to come out grief-free on the other side. It feels more like being a ping pong ball in a shoe box that gets bumped around without warning.

While we know that major milestones like holidays are potential triggers of divorce grief, there can be daily reminders of the loss. For example, cleaning out a drawer and coming across last year's Christmas card, running into intact families at the park, or hearing your wedding song in the produce section. Just when you thought you were okay, something knocks you right back.

Surrendering to the grief when it arises becomes part of moving through it. You might need to spend five minutes crying in your car after the first parent–teacher conference. A fun night with friends might be punctuated with teary eyes and requests for hugs. A solo night indulging in a comedy special may conclude with a puddle of snot and tears. Divorce grief arises when it wants, and it's our job to honor it as part of the process.

RITUALS OF GRIEF

Society offers few rituals for marking the end of a marriage, leaving couples to navigate this territory largely on their own. Rituals can provide structure for processing grief and marking transitions. I encourage my clients to design a closing ritual for themselves. One client chose to gather close friends to witness the removal of her wedding band, followed by a fascinating discussion about what to do with it. Another popular ritual is a giant bonfire, good for turning the past to ash. Another couple had a Getting Un-married Ceremony (together!) and invited their extended community. Their logic being: they were married with the support of their friends, why would their divorce be any different.

Without such markers, divorce can feel like a gradual fade rather than a significant life passage. In the absence of marking the marriage's end and the beginning of the next chapter, people can get stuck in the spin cycle of their life and future relationships. When people waste precious moments in conflict with their co-parent or ruminate on the past, it's like constantly picking at a scab. Stop picking! It's the only way it will stop bleeding and scar over. Scars remind us that we came through something difficult and survived. But it no longer hurts.

Be gentle with yourself and, if possible, with your former partner. Allow space for grief amid the spreadsheets and schedules. Remember that sadness isn't a sign you're making the wrong choice—it's simply acknowledgment of the significance of what's ending. Even the most necessary endings need time to be mourned.

Creating meaning from the loss can also help transform pain into an integrated experience. This involves acknowledging that the relationship held value, despite the fact it didn't last to the end of our lives. The years spent in a relationship aren't wasted; they are a valuable environment for personal growth. The children born from the union are precious. The lessons learned have shaped who we are and will become. Finding meaning allows divorcing people to hold multiple truths at once, such as the marriage needed to end *and* the marriage mattered.

IN THEIR OWN WORDS

The Good Divorce Show
Season 3, Episode 4
Ellen, 2 daughters (19 & 23)
Married 31 Years – Divorced 15

Listen to the full episode here:

WORKING TOGETHER

Karen: Well, let's go back in time when the "D" word finally gets spoken. And what I refer to as the messy middle. Are we in? Are we out? Should we stay together? We're trying. Let's go to counseling. Let's try this. I think so many of us struggle with just making the decision. You and your former spouse were no different. Would you mind pulling back the curtain a little bit on your family?

Ellen: Well, first I would say that we all get married thinking that's our life going forward. When all of a sudden, you find yourself in a position where there's not a lot of forward thinking going on, in terms of what you and your partner are going to be; there's just a stall that happens in life.

I have always said that there's three ways it can go. You can either stay steady and stay the course, sort of suck it up and carry on. Or you're a lucky one, and a recalibration happens, and you reclaim a way of moving forward that is different and mutually beneficial. Or you get divorced. It feels like there's three ways to go.

Karen: I would echo that as well.

Ellen: Yeah, so something had happened to change the dynamic of our relationship, where each one of us was going inward in our own way to deal with whatever it was we were facing, rather than trying to come together and find a different solution or find a different way.

And so the difficulty was, we were both very family-oriented. Both of us really cared about what we had built together. There was always mutual respect and deep love. So, it's hard to even imagine saying this isn't working anymore.

Karen: Did you have the notion to "stay for the kids"?

Ellen: Yes, that was also something, in the back of my mind, that I always found curious; if you then stick it out for the kids, you're modeling a mediocre core relationship for them. I think to the extent that you can be honest with yourself and honest with your partner and reflect that, that's a huge part of any relationship even if it's not working. The kids need to be able to see that process.

I never had any reason to doubt my relationship; I never had any reason to not trust or any desire not to be married. And then all of a sudden, I am faced with what's happening. It was very much a surprise.

Karen: What would you say to a listener right now, who is in those early days of what they might be feeling, and some things that they could consider doing in order to help move through all the feelings?

Ellen: Well, one of the things that took me by surprise is just how big my grief was. Maybe I was at an age in my life where it was safe to let myself feel grief. But the grief that came pouring out was much bigger than the divorce. And I was quite taken back by this surge of grief that just kind of overwhelmed me.

And then I realized that I was grieving certain aspects of my childhood. I had experienced the death of a fiancé in my early twenties. That those—when I was little as a child and when I was 20—it was not a … I didn't have the resources, or the support, or the safety net to really feel that grief. And I kind of just pushed through and, you know, jam on with life, because you're 20 and everybody around you is having a good time. Nobody's really going to be that empathetic or sensitive to your grief. And so, you just carry on.

Well, at 55, it all just came flying out. I really was afraid to just surrender to the feelings. It felt like too big of an abyss. One day, I just let go. And it's like, well, what's gonna happen? Am I gonna be in the fetal position on my bed for the rest of my life?

But I just gave myself complete permission to be in that—to feel it. And I was sure I'd feel like I was falling down the rabbit hole, but then all of a sudden there was a different energy, sort of an updraft, if you will. And I went, huh, I don't have to hang onto the edge here. I can surrender and feel this, and something else rises.

And that was probably the first time in my life that I got that feeling, like, you're not gonna die, if you feel so deeply.

Karen: I would appreciate you chatting with our listeners about having young adult kids. It's not like you're done, "Now we're divorced, and we don't have to co-parent anymore." Because I know 18 to 25 years old—that period—they're still trying to get through college, and get financially secure, and find their solid job and long-term relationships. So, there's still a lot of parenting going on.

And sometimes, when we divorce after the kids are out of high school, especially during that last stage of adolescence, 18–25, the family doesn't really have a rule book.

Ellen: We didn't have a parenting plan. We didn't have a schedule of where to spend the holidays. We didn't know how to operate as a divorced family.

Karen: So, how did you and your children, and their father, begin to navigate this new territory with young adults who still needed co-parenting?

Ellen: Well, you know, it's messy. And you do the best you can. My older daughter moved, and she was on the East Coast. So, she had more distance to it. And my younger daughter was going to college in the same town that we lived in. And I think that may have been hard on her.

It was a very clear decision, probably on both of our parts, to maintain the role of co-parent, and to keep a solid front for them in that regard.

Karen: You and your husband had worked together for years. So, what happened on that front postdivorce?

Ellen: When I really knew the divorce was happening, and that ultimate separation of our marriage was going to be absolute, I took another leave of absence. At that time, I applied for a new job in healthcare that I had every qualification for. I had the application completely done, and I was going to send it online, and I just took a pause. At that moment, I did sort of an inventory about what was important to me. Was I running? Was I just looking for a different job to get out of there? Or how was this different job going to serve me and my goals and values?

So, when I was going to apply for this other job, it was full-time. I needed that, for the financial salary and health benefits and all of that. I realized I don't want to step back into not having the flexibility and the quality of work life that I had at the firm. So, I didn't send in the job application. That's when I knew I had to recalibrate myself. I let myself wonder if everything about me had to change? Can my job stay the same? Because it's good for me. It's beneficial. It's benefiting me in many ways.

Karen: But it would require you to work alongside your former spouse. So, you really did have to recalibrate and make a decision and a commitment to go back.

Ellen: Correct. Yeah. So, I chose not to go looking for other jobs. I developed consulting work for other law offices on the side. It was very pressurized, and I didn't have the working relationship, or the dialogue with the attorneys along the way, that helps everything unfold more smoothly. So, as time went by, I decided I would simply stay at the law firm my ex-husband owned.

Karen: Was it a conversation you had with your former spouse around new boundaries, or how you would operate in the office? Or was it just business as usual?

Ellen: We didn't really have a conversation about it. I really strove for neutrality while I was at work. I kept in touch with how I was feeling and was very private about it, maintaining neutrality and professionalism to the extent I could at work. That gave kind of everyone permission to just carry on. There's something kind of soothing about that too. People were kind. They gave me time and space. I think they appreciated the neutrality and being able to just do the work.

Karen: I'm here to say compartmentalization can be very beneficial and appropriate. You and your former spouse found a way to manage that at work. How did your personal relationship evolve over that decade of working side by side but not being married?

Ellen: Well, one of the benefits of interfacing with my ex-spouse on a routine basis is there were times where his behavior or personality was just shining in all its glory, and I could just sit back and think—I am a lucky woman to not be married to that anymore.

I remember saying to my ex, right as we were going to the courthouse to get the divorce finalized, that while in truth I maybe wished he lived on another planet, I was going to choose love. It was a decision that I made right at the juncture when the gavel came down. I chose love. And I think all along the way, it's love, respect, and forgiveness—whether it's forgiving the partner for whatever happened or forgiving yourself—and then just holding that for yourself, for your ex, and even your kids.

Karen: Would you describe for us what that relationship looks like today? You, the father of your children, what do you anticipate now that you are retired, and don't work together? How would you describe it?

Ellen: Well, we started our relationship way back in the day as really good friends. I would say that's still the state of our relationship. If I am in trouble, he is still a person I can call. He actually has become my biggest support for taking care of my dog when I want to travel. We help each other in ways that are meaningful and substantive. It's good. We need all the friends we can have in life. A piece of advice I had been given was, instead of looking for ways he is no longer supporting you, focus on the ways he is still supporting you. That was helpful and really reminded me of the friendship piece of it. So, yeah, we're friends.

CHAPTER SEVEN

THE COMMUNITY

REFLECTION: INTO THE LIGHT

Six weeks after David and I decided to divorce, I was still in the raw, immediate aftermath of separation, and also still in my pajamas and barely functional most days. That's when we really need our circle of support to show up, and my circle really showed up for me. Two of my besties descended on my house on a Thursday afternoon, scooped me up off my couch, and helped me see some light in the darkness.

"Pack your knickers, McNenny, we're taking a road trip," came Lydia's well-rehearsed chaperone directive. "We are going over the hills, and through the woods to Diwali."

"What's Diwali? And what if my kids need me over the weekend? I don't think I should leave town," came my resistant and uncertain response.

"That's why they have a father," came Hazel's deadpan West Virginia twang. She wasn't wrong. I was still adjusting to the idea of part-time parenting.

They were headed to a Diwali party in North Idaho. Their longtime friend, Larry, subscribed to the "Hindu-for-a-Day" philosophy and had been hosting this special event for 30 years. Hazel and Lydia decided this should be my single-lady coming out party. I barely knew the hosts and was certain a divorcing depressed mom was the last guest anyone would want to hang out with. My friends assured me I'd be welcome with open arms; both Larry and his wife, Katrina, had come through divorce and then found each other. Their 26 years together were a testament to finding love and joy, postdivorce. I didn't know it then, but they would become an important lighthouse in the landscape of divorce.

I was too exhausted from wallowing to put up a fight. I packed my bags, and we headed west.

Diwali marks the Hindu New Year. The hosts stuck to the traditional custom of sharing a vegetarian meal with friends, in the glow of nothing but candlelight. There were candles on the tables, in the windows, even the roof was outlined in candlelight. Little flames everywhere, flickering in protest against the encroaching autumnal darkness. It was a stunning sight.

I was introduced to the other guests—a mix of local friends, neighbors, and a few out-of-towners. There were about 20 of us in total. This was my first social event since David and I publicly announced news of our divorce a few months ago. That news felt a little more exposing and vulnerable back home, but here, tonight, no one knew my story. I didn't have to be that woman going through a divorce. I could just be Karen.

But I actually couldn't be just Karen, I was divorcing Karen. The turmoil I was navigating consumed me and the space around me. I was unable to compartmentalize the events of my life from the events of the evening.

I proceeded to dominate virtually every cocktail conversation. I talked about my divorce, asked if they were divorced, did they have advice, and how damaged were the children? Barbara Walters took over my brain, and I started to see divorce as a shared experience that's not often talked about. Certainly not talked about in a positive context, because the narrative around divorce is pretty damn dark and depressing. There was comfort in hearing people's stories; it provided solace, support, and hope.

I sat in the warmth of the fire on the flagstone hearth, letting my entire back be wrapped in a warm blanket. Nothing can replace the percussion of burning wood, which transported sweet winter aroma throughout the room. Sitting next to me was Jacki who had been married 23 years, divorced 12, and had 2 adult children.

She punctuated our conversation with these words: "Sadly, it takes most of us a long time to realize most of the crap we're all worked up about really doesn't matter. Certainly, the battle could have been avoided." I turned to face her straight on, not wanting to miss a word. "During my most painful days when there was still a lot of conflict and I was bitching up a storm about this and that, my girlfriend turned to me on a dog walk and said, 'Do you want to be right, or make it right? Which matters more to you?'" Her words hit a tuning fork in my head.

The guests, rather than pity me, were gracious and supportive. I had effectively turned the Diwali celebration into group therapy for myself, and it made a world of difference. In the dark of the night, the party filled the outside deck overlooking the cliffs of Lake Pend Oreille under a canopy of stars, each of us with Larry's signature Manhattan drink in hand.

Never missing an opportunity to make a toast, Larry gathered us together, "Thank you for coming! Diwali is one of the few Hindu holidays universally celebrated around the world. In the Southern hemisphere, it is the celebration of Latchmi, the Goddess of light and prosperity, taking place when the days are getting longer and spring crops are coming to life. It is when spring cleaning takes place in the homes, the manure piles are spread on the fields, everyone gets new clothing, and the kids get extra candy. A happy, exciting holiday! So, drink up; start the feast; and may your year be filled with good health, light, and prosperity!"

The entire weekend was filled with rich conversation, laughs, long walks, and support. There was a moment where I felt … okay. I had the fleeting sense that this overwhelming grief wasn't permanent. The disorientation, the sense that I was starting over, and the immense worry and guilt about what this divorce would do to my children, lifted momentarily. The tension in my shoulders left, and I could breathe using my whole chest. Diwali offered up light for my future.

CIRCLE OF SUPPORT

I'd always had a hard time being alone. Even before David, I'd filled my life with constant activities and people, on top of working full-time. The divorce left me with too much time alone. As I grieved, I leaned into my people. They knew me before David, before kids, and so I sensed they would help me re-know myself postdivorce.

Writer Maggie Smith noted, "… when you lose 'your person,' it's critical to have 'your people.'"[1] My friends were the people I could rely on for emotional support. There's a sense of emotional security that

---

[1] Smith, Maggie. (2023). During my divorce, close friends became a parachute. *New York Times* (May 5, 2023). https://www.nytimes.com/2023/05/05/well/mind/divorce-healing-friendship.html.

comes with good friends. I knew there was almost nothing I could do that would drive them away, and vice versa. Being able to lean into that unbreakable bond reminded me of what a healthy functioning relationship could look like.

My friend, Elizabeth, was one of those shoulders I cried on. I'd call her when the grief felt too big to contain, and she'd simply listen while I sobbed into the phone.

"I'm supposed to be strong," I remember saying, one rough evening. "I'm the one who decided on this divorce. I shouldn't be falling apart."

"Says who?" Elizabeth's voice was gentle but firm through the phone. "You're allowed to grieve. You're allowed to be a mess. Stop working to convince everyone, and yourself, that everything is all bubbles and rainbows. It's a shit sandwich, we all know that, so just eat it and feel what you're feeling." She connected me to the heavy reality of my new life and gave me the permission slip I needed to fall apart, at least every now and then.

TELLING THE PARENTS

My fear of telling the kids was rivaled only by my fear of talking to my parents. Not that they would be mean-spirited or angry, but I knew they would be heartbroken. It was all just so unpleasant for everyone.

The evening after our final conversation with Esther, we sat at our kitchen table after the kids were in bed. The house was quiet except for the faint sound of the dishwasher running in the background. I had a legal pad in front of me, filled with notes and to-do lists—my version of a security blanket.

We decided that before we told Anya and Dwyer, we needed to spread the news to the other adults in their lives—their circle of support and ours. Our kids shouldn't be the ones having to tell their teacher or their aunt that their parents are divorcing. We made a list, including neighbors on our street, Dwyer's preschool teacher, Anya's second-grade teacher, our babysitters, and the playdate parents. People who would need to know, so they could support the kids through the transition and not get blindsided by the news.

"I guess we should start with our immediate families this week," I sighed.

"I'll take mine; you take yours?" David suggested.

"Yup," I put a check mark on the list next to *Tell Families*. "I'll call the schools tomorrow and get time to set up to meet with both teachers."

Most of my siblings lived out of town, so those conversations would be phone calls. But my parents, I knew I had to see them in person.

The conversation went about how I'd anticipated. Mom and Dad, people of deep religious faith who had "stuck it out" despite their own underwhelming marriage, struggled to understand our decision. I sat in their living room, the same room where I'd once played as a child, and I watched their faces fall as I shared our news.

"Are you sure?" my mother was tearful, "Have you tried everything?"

I explained that we had indeed tried—three therapists over eight years wasn't exactly giving up easily.

"Could you stick it out for the kids?" my father added, echoing the same Catholic philosophy that had kept him in his marriage.

"We're going to do everything in our power to make sure this doesn't negatively impact Anya and Dwyer," I assured them, beginning to understand a bit of what Esther was getting at with the "do no more harm" advice. "Their well-being is our number-one priority."

"We love you, and we love those grandkids," Mom said, squeezing my hand. I know her greatest worry was for *her* grandkids. That's often where the heart of a grandparent goes. She didn't say it, but I know what she was thinking, "So help me God, if you screw up my grandchildren and destroy their childhood, I will never forgive you."

THE OUTLAWS

I have always felt welcome and a sense of belonging in David's family, maybe even more than my own. We all shared the same love of dance, music, and community-making. I didn't want those relationships to disappear because our marriage had ended. My sister-in-law and I had been friends before we married brothers. Would I have to break up with her too? Our four kids were close in age and were literally growing up together. Would the family play dates continue? Would I still be invited to any gatherings?

David's mother lived out of town, and even though we didn't see her regularly, she and I developed a close relationship, independent of David. She would tell me, "You are the daughter of my heart, Karen." For all I know, this is the sort of adoration she would shower on just about anyone. It didn't matter, because she meant it every time. She embodied peace, love and joy, and had plenty to go around.

"From the beginning, I was worried about the gaps between you," she had told me during our first visit after announcing the divorce. She'd seen what I was only beginning to acknowledge—that love alone wasn't enough to bridge fundamental incompatibilities. And who knew this man better than his mother? "I understand the struggle between you. Of course, I wish your marriage wasn't ending, like mine did to his father. But I trust the two of you will do a beautiful job raising your children together."

After the divorce, I was able to visit my mother-in-law a couple more times before she was diagnosed with pancreatic cancer. She wasn't the kind of person who prioritized her health or saw health-conscious decisions as a worthwhile endeavor. It wasn't a surprise when she announced she wasn't interested in treatment of any kind. She chose to live fully to the end, without medical intervention, which came within weeks of the diagnosis.

I knew the cancer was rapidly progressing, and that before too long, she was at the hospital under palliative care. The end was imminent. To his credit,

David reached out and granted me permission to come see his mother before she died. I was so grateful. All of this was happening during the first year of living separately. Everything was still so tender, and we were navigating all sorts of new territory. I certainly wasn't expecting a double dose of loss and grief.

I was full of anxiety and fear when I arrived at the hospital. I would see all of his family at their mother's bedside, as she was dying. I meandered through the fluorescent hallways, looking for the right room. When I finally found her room, I took a deep breath, held it, and gently pushed open the door. A wash of beautiful harmonies and warm tones cascaded into my soul, and I exhaled. Of course, they were circled up around the bed, arms wrapped around each other, singing a shower of love over their mother's bed.

The youngest son and his wife looked up and acknowledged my arrival. Without missing a note, they opened the circle and made room for me between their arms. Their warm embrace gave me the reassurance I was seeking. I was so grateful the loving spirit of David's family made space for me and my heart to grieve alongside them. Through their mother, we were all reminded that family transcends death and divorce.

DON'T ASK WHY

When it comes to divorce, people act as though it might be contagious or assume the divorcing couple doesn't want to talk about it. As a result, there's a tendency to ignore or resist divorce grief, both for the persons going through it, and for the community surrounding the couple. Friends and family don't often ask, because it's presumed to be a private matter, and we are generally underskilled at having deep relationship conversations with each other. Consequently, divorce often resides in a cave of shame and silence.

However, there's no harm in asking people how they are doing, just don't ask "Why?". I have found most people find it helpful to talk about what they are going through but resist because they don't want to make others uncomfortable or dominate the conversation. Here's a secret though: it's not prying to ask *how* someone is doing and if they need support. It is prying if you want to know *why* they are getting divorced.

Whether amicable or contentious, divorce is hard. The end of a marriage (or any partnership) is a life transition deserving of care and support. The grief that comes with divorce is real and valid, and all too often people confuse their natural feelings of loss and mourning with feelings of shame. This legacy of shame keeps many couples silent, suffering alone rather than reaching out for help. This silence only reinforces the stigma, creating a cycle where divorce remains taboo because no one talks about it, and no one talks about it because it's taboo.

By being forthright about divorce with others, we create a network of support to sustain us through the difficult transition. Friends may offer help with childcare. Colleagues may give us more grace when productivity wanes, or when we need additional time off to manage the business of divorce. In my situation, our children's teachers were aware so they could provide extra emotional support during school hours, understanding that the kids might need additional patience or reassurance. Had we tried to keep our separation clandestine, we would've denied ourselves these crucial support systems at a time when we needed them most.

Consistency for our children was another benefit of our transparency. When children sense there's a family secret, it creates an undue burden that can manifest as anxiety, confusion, or behavioral issues. By being open about our divorce with the adults in our children's lives, we ensured that Anya and Dwyer received the same message and support regardless of where they were. They didn't have to worry about accidentally revealing our "secret" or navigating different truths in different environments. Instead, they could focus on their own process of adjustment, secure in the knowledge that the adults around them understood what they were going through.

Perhaps most importantly, our openness offered an alternative model for others to consider. Just as I had sought out examples of divorce during our struggling years, I wanted to be open in case there was someone else out there looking for proof that separation didn't have to be destructive. Breaking the silence around divorce doesn't just help the couple in question—it chips away at the stigma for everyone, creating more space for honest conversations about the complex reality of relationships. Each time someone chooses openness over secrecy, they add another point of light to guide others through what can be a dark and lonely passage. In being transparent about our journey, I was starting to contribute, in a small way, to a more compassionate understanding of divorce in our community.

STAY AHEAD OF THE PRESS

I once heard a journalist advise, "Stay ahead of the press. Write your own headlines." They were talking about a public relations tactic to keep gossip at bay regarding a well-known figurehead. However, it suddenly made good sense regarding our concerns about gossip and our family story. Not only did David and I implement this tactic, I now share it with other families as part of The Good Divorce Method.

In Chapter 3, I outlined a thoughtful process for talking to the kids. It's worth considering a similar approach for other areas of your life. This is the same advice I have been giving to my business clients for over 25 years: "When employees don't have information, they make it up. And what they make up is usually worse than the truth."

Our circle of support does not necessarily know how to support us, so they often become scarce when we need them the most. But we can take on the responsibility to educate, inform, and guide. I suggest writing a Public Service Announcement (PSA) for your shared community. In doing so, couples are empowered to write the narrative *before* the gossip mill takes over and writes it for them.

In addition to what I outlined in Chapter 4, for younger kiddos, I also suggest reaching out to the parents of close friends. It is hard to predict when, if, or to whom your kids will share the news of your divorce. In one case, a six-year-old child was playing house with their bestie and suggested that they "play divorce." This led to a discussion between the kids, which led to a conversation between the bestie and their parents, and then a phone call to the divorcing parents … well, you can see the cascade effect. Young kids might leap to conclusions and concerns about their own parents, "Are you getting divorced?" By providing a heads up, you give everyone a better chance of being prepared and successful with their own kids.

The other place a communication plan might be applicable is in your professional life. I certainly encourage clients to communicate with their immediate supervisor, and maybe even their co-workers, as to what is going on. Most of us find it hard to make a slice of toast while navigating divorce, let alone show up as our most productive person at work. If the couple owns a business together, having a strategic communication plan is essential. The last thing a business owner wants is for employees to dust off their resumes and run for the hills based on a rumor.

THE GOOD GUIDE: DIVORCE PUBLIC SERVICE ANNOUNCEMENT

Hello friends and family,

You may have already heard that we have made the really difficult decision to divorce. We wanted to let you know that we have no interest in blowing up our family or engaging in a drawn-out legal battle. In fact, we are working with ____________ to guide us through a thoughtful and compassionate process. We are grateful we won't be lawyering up and going to court.

We haven't talked to the kids yet, so we appreciate you keeping this news to yourself for the time being. We would hate for our children to hear this news secondhand from anyone, including one of their friends. We intend to talk to them this week, once we have a few more ducks in a row. We will let you know when that conversation has taken place.

We appreciate your love and support during this difficult time and don't want anyone to feel like they need to "take sides." We are both on Team (child's name) and ask you to do the same. We also ask for your discretion as you honor our privacy about such a personal issue. But there's no need to avoid us in the produce section. Please don't ask us why we're getting separated, but feel free to ask how we're doing, or if there is anything we need.

* * * * * * * *

To our valued employees,
We are sorry to relay the news that we have made the very difficult decision to enter into the divorce process. Although this is a big shift in our private life, we intend to work together on behalf of the business. We wanted to let you know that we have no interest in doing damage to our family or engaging in a drawn-out legal battle. In fact, we are working with ___________ to guide us through a thoughtful and compassionate process. We are so grateful we can keep our child(ren) centered in our decisions and protect their future moving forward. We intend to do the same for the business.

We appreciate your support and patience during this difficult time. We don't want anyone to feel like they should be "taking sides," we are all on Team-(business name). We also ask for your discretion as you honor our privacy about such a personal issue. No need to ask us why we're getting separated, but feel free to ask how we're doing, or if there is anything we need. We want you to feel secure in our ability to continue supporting you and the business.

WHO GETS THE CHURCH?

Many couples will feel the urge to divvy up their community spaces, sometimes even down to the hours a former partner can go to the gym, or what days of the week they can go to a favorite coffee shop. Part of this is due to a scarcity mindset creeping in, which is so prevalent in a divorce process. Not to mention, seeing a former partner unexpectedly can stir up big emotions in the early wake of a divorce. Maybe having some boundaries around shared spaces makes sense, for a time. But as weeks and months pass, we want to be sturdy enough to weather the awkward, contentious, or sad interactions triggered by a former partner. To echo Esther, we want to become indifferent. Not unfriendly or unkind, just less triggered with fewer expectations of each other.

A friend, also going through divorce, came to me completely outraged when her husband declared, "You know, I'm taking the church."

"He's taking the church?" I said, completely disoriented by her comment, "What does that even mean?"

"It means he wants to attend *our* church with *our* kids," she replied, crossing her arms, "and I'm supposed to find someplace else."

I reflected back to her, "I was under the impression that you weren't really *churchy people*."

"Exactly, which makes this all the more ridiculous," she clarified. "We started going because the pastor agreed to marry us, and then we just kept going because … I don't know, it seemed like the right thing to do with the kids."

"Are you telling me he can't tolerate your presence in the same sanctuary? Doesn't sound very Christian to me." I was heartbroken for my friend.

"Correct me if I'm wrong, but I don't think he gets to have that kind of control over me—banning me from public places!" She was at her wit's end and unwilling to agree to this or any other division of public spaces. Frankly, I agreed.

This wasn't a sensible foundation for a good divorce. Plus, they lived in a small town, not Manhattan; it's not like there were a lot of choices for her. She was also concerned about being cut out of her children's religious path. Her mind was swirling with unanswered questions: *What would happen on Sunday mornings when they were in her home? Was she "allowed" to take them on those days? Would he insist on picking up the kids for church, regardless of the schedule?* I could see they were off course and a course correction was needed sooner than later. I suggested she go talk with her pastor about the situation and see if he had any insights.

Two weeks later, she shared what unfolded with the pastor. "I shared with him how ridiculous my ex was being. It was more like presenting my case, hoping he would be my agreeable judge and jury. He sat and listened to all of it, because he is a good pastor. The whole thing was so ironic. Here I was, talking to the man who married us about my divorce problems." I was able to laugh with my girlfriend over the absurdity of it all.

In the end, the pastor didn't take my friend's side, or her ex's. He simply reminded her that there was an early service at 9:00 and a later service at 10:30. "Some parents choose to attend different services. Sadly, this does happen and sometimes we lose the family altogether."

They sorted things out so the residential parent would take the kids to church. For the most part, neither of them bothered to even go to the early service on their own. Eventually, after enough missed services, because of family conflicts or kid activities, they both realized that church wasn't going to be a focal point for their family. They both softened their grip, and the church slowly faded away within a couple of years. All that wasted time and energy over a thing that didn't really matter to either of them in the end.

Of course, we all know that the conflict was never about the church. Seldom is the conflict about *the thing;* it's almost always about loss of control and an attempt to regain power. Like colonial powers drawing borders and falsely claiming sovereignty over different territories, divorcing partners can get caught up in dividing the landscapes they inhabit. We're so consumed with *dividing up* the stuff of life that we forget there are some aspects of life we may still have to *share*.

PICKING SIDES

The expectation for most divorcing couples is that not only do belongings, assets, and children get divided, but so do friends and family members. When a relationship ends, partners will sometimes try to stake claim to certain people. They might deny access to family members or shared friends. Regretfully, for a period of time, I also fell into this trap. During the long gauntlet of divorce, I needed my family to be on my side of the fence supporting me. I didn't want any familial generosity flowing his way. It was such a waste of love on my part.

In the most heartbreaking cases, partners begin to speak poorly about their former spouses, airing all the dirty laundry to their shared community in hopes of creating loyalties in their favor. Dividing up the people in our lives is inadvisable. Often, friends feel torn in this awkward position of having to choose sides. When a relationship ends, particularly one as intense as a marriage, we need external relationships to buoy us.

It was a new framework for our family. For instance, Dwyer's closest friend, George, and his family had been part of our lives since the boys were toddlers, but suddenly they didn't know the protocol. Who do you call about a playdate when the parents live in different houses? Which house do you send the birthday party invitation to? Do you need to invite both parents, and if so, is that going to be uncomfortable for everyone?

I noticed some families simply retreated, unsure how to navigate the new dynamics. The invitations stopped coming, not due to malice but confusion. So, I started having explicit conversations, providing some guidance to our community.

"Just treat us like you always have," I said. "Send a text to both of us. We're still Dwyer's parents, just with different addresses. Don't worry about knowing our schedule—just reach out the way you always have, and we will take it from there."

"Oh, okay, got it," Wren said, when I spelled it out. "We wanted to include Dwyer in George's camping birthday party, but Gus and I spent twenty minutes debating how to handle the invitation. Do we send two? Do we call? Do we ask you to ask David? It felt like a minefield."

It seemed so simple, once we talked about it. But without that explicit permission, families often become paralyzed with concern of doing the wrong thing and may choose to avoid the situation altogether.

The pressure to divide our social world came from surprising directions. Even though my friends were clearly "mine," some still felt compelled to demonstrate loyalty by cutting David out entirely. "I unfriended him on Facebook," one friend announced proudly, as if she'd struck a blow for justice. Well-meaning acquaintances would lower their voices at school events to ask, "Is it okay that we still talk to David?" I did my best to reassure those who asked that it was expected they would still be in contact with both me and David, particularly if it regarded our kids. We discovered that we had to retrain and educate our community that this wasn't a battleground, and they didn't need to soldier-up for either of us.

WORDS MATTER

As a business consultant, facilitator, and mediator, I've spent decades witnessing how language shapes reality. I knew from countless observations how a single word could shift an entire conversation, how reframing a statement could transform conflict into collaboration. So, when David and I decided to separate, this professional understanding became deeply personal. Every phrase, label, and casual reference has the power to wound and divide or to heal and unite. I was determined to use language that would help our family remain a family.

The language of divorce is loaded, so I made some adjustments to my language, starting with "ex." Perhaps no word in the divorce lexicon carries more baggage than "ex." The "ex-" prefix itself implies something rejected or finished. For some people, this terminology doesn't carry negative weight, but in much of Western culture, "ex" is loaded with implications of heartbreak, bitterness, dislike, and even malice.

X-ING THE EX

I couldn't bring myself to refer to David as my "ex-husband," that felt hostile. He wasn't my ex-anything; he was my children's father, my co-parent, my former spouse. He was still very much present in my life, just in a different role. David and I had a forever relationship, and as long as we were raising kids together, "ex" felt too dismissive of the family we created and the kids we were raising together.

When we were married, there was a little cocktail banter we often used. "Oh, hello Robert, have you met David, my first husband?" and we would all have a chuckle about the implications of referring to my *current* husband as my *first* husband. So, after we divorced, I decided to stick with it. I sometimes still refer to David as my "dear first husband." People quickly assume he is dead or that I have remarried. "Nope, he's still alive, just not my husband anymore. And there's only been one … so far." It still gets a chuckle, and I feel better about myself when I can speak about him in a warm and lighthearted manner. He will always be my first.

RENOVATING "BROKEN"

Another term I rejected was *broken home* or *fractured home*. These phrases imply division and damage, even failure. Instead, as I mentioned in Chapter 5, we are "one family, living across two homes." I never wanted Anya and Dwyer to internalize the idea that they were somehow incomplete or damaged because their parents discovered they were incompatible as spouses. Children absorb the language adults use about them and their circumstances, often carrying those labels into adulthood. If everyone around them spoke (or whispered) of their broken home/family, they might eventually see themselves as broken in some way, a term I hope my children never assign to themselves.

The term *renovation* became central to how I explained our families' transformation. We were taking parts of our family and arranging them differently to better serve our new needs. Anyone who has ever been through a major house renovation knows it's painful, inconvenient, and often takes longer and costs more than you want it to, like divorce. But in the end, we suffer through it in the name of improvement.

POWER HOUR

Beyond providing emotional support, my friends were also there when I needed practical help. The moms in my neighborhood had a standing agreement that we could call for a "Power Hour" anytime. It was like Batman's *bat signal* for weary moms, and as a newly minted single parent, I was definitely weary. All I had to do was send out a text with my request; Not for an entire day or a weekend, but just for one powerful hour of support. Whoever could make it would show up ready to do whatever needed doing, be it scrubbing the bathroom, yard work, or folding piles of laundry. As the saying goes, "Many hands make light work."

Two months after David moved out, I called for a Power Hour. But this time around, it wasn't the moms I wanted; I needed their handy husbands. I asked the ladies if I could borrow their hubbies. I had a list of household fixes I needed done and lacked the time, skills, and resources to do them all myself. My girlfriends happened to marry a gaggle of handy dudes with tools, who they were more than happy to share with me. And all those great hubbies said "Yes."

Late on a Wednesday night, five husbands arrived on my doorstep with their tools. I'd made detailed lists for each person, complete with instructions, and all necessary supplies onsite. Part of the success of any Power Hour was being prepared for the crew. I had beer in the cooler and pizza on the counter when they arrived. It probably wasn't necessary, but I wanted them to know I was grateful, and words didn't seem like enough.

"Where do you want me?" asked Peter, toolbox in hand and a grin on his face.

"I've got assignments," I said, holding up a spreadsheet I'd prepped. Soon the house filled with the sounds of productive work. Stuart tackled the light fixture over the stairs and dining table. Tim replaced the downstairs toilet while Allen changed out the upstairs toilet. Peter followed me to the bedroom where I had already painted the walls, rearranged the furniture, and bought a new mattress and fresh bedding. The final touch was to replace the old light fixture with a crystal chandelier I had in storage. He also helped me with the double-wide rod for the new curtains I wanted to hang. Reclaiming my bedroom was essential.

Within one hour, my list was conquered. It was amazing! We sat around my kitchen table, eating pizza and drinking beer just long enough for a group of guys to get uncomfortable sitting around with a divorceé, unsure what to say. I swiftly sent them home to their wives.

A strange silver lining appeared in the midst of leaning on my friends during the divorce—they leaned back. When I made the first Power Hour request of my girlfriends, it opened the gates for others to ask for what they needed. As they left my house that day, everyone was thanking *me*, "Because you were courageous enough to ask for help, Karen, now we feel like we can too." I used to think I had to do everything on my own to be an adult, but during my divorce, as I navigated lows, I realized being a functioning adult meant embracing the interdependence of supportive relationships.

IN THEIR OWN WORDS

The Good Divorce Show
Season 1, Episode 4
Elke, 10 years old at time of divorce
Recorded 40 years postdivorce

Listen to the full episode here:

BONUS PARENTS

Karen: I've heard some kids say they can feel like a ping-pong ball, going back and forth between two places.

Elke: I think that's a reason why we've been a functional family. Our family has always been very centered on the kids, because it's very centered on being good parents, and that has remained my entire life. I'm sure there were side channels and compromises that I wasn't aware of. But from where I sat, it was pretty seamless. I can remember friends all through growing up that had divorced parents who couldn't have dinner together, or they had to have two graduation parties. And we never, ever had that.

Karen: As you sit and reflect on that now as an adult, as a parent yourself in a long-term marriage, what would you say to your parents by way of appreciation or advice, and how they did it in those early years?

Elke: Oh, that's a great question. I definitely appreciate never having to choose one over the other. No one was ever badmouthing
each other. I'm super grateful for that. What I would acknowledge is, how much I didn't know—at least for me. When I had
my own children, I remember looking at my mom one day and
being like, oh my God, you were just trying your best all the time,
weren't you? That is the theme of parenting. But I don't think
I really got that. I think as a child, it's easy to keep thinking, "well,
why would you do this?" You are sure your parents are doing this
wrong, you know? Now that I have teenagers and I'm getting
some of that same feedback, I'm thinking to myself, "you don't
even know how hard I'm trying." I'm literally trying to help you
all the time. I can look at my parents now with so much more
empathy. And because they weren't sharing all that complexity
with us or asking us to carry it for them, life was better. I mean,
there was conflict, clearly, and there were times when there were
disagreements. I remember arguments and fights and things, but
they never broke the family.

Karen: How did traditions change, events, activities, birthdays,
Christmases?

Elke: When we were all living in the same town, nothing really
changed. We still all had holidays together. There wasn't Dad's
Christmas and Mom's Christmas. I think that decision, however
they came to it, and I don't know if they had a counselor or someone guiding them, but however they came to that decision, they
really stuck to it.

Karen: And this was in the 1970s, when divorce had a lot of hang-ups.
You were probably more of a minority as a divorced kid in school.
It was more rare. In so many ways, your parents were radical. They
were pioneers. Around age 10, there was a shift in the family.

Elke: Yes. My mother reconnected with her high school sweetheart.
He heard about my parent's divorce and started showing up a
little bit, then a little more. And eventually, they decided to get

married, but he was still living in Alaska, and we were in Montana. So, the decision was made to spend a summer in Alaska and see how that went. We spent a summer there, came back and did a school year, and then moved to Alaska the following year.

When I first moved to Alaska, I really missed Montana. I missed my best friend. I missed my dad. I was one of those kids who was resistant to change. I was very much the "you're not my real dad" kid. "You can't tell me what to do." And so, he got a book about being a stepparent. The two core ideas that he took from that book were, "Don't expect anything for two years" and "They just need to know you are there." He closed the book and committed to it. His second lesson, "They just need to know you're there," he is still deeply committed to that. He's always my first call when I need help or need ideas or to talk something through.

Karen: I've heard you talk about your stepfather, Tom, being "your person" and what it's like to have a bonus parent in your life.

Elke: Yes, I am really fortunate that more than two people were carrying the load, or [having] two perspectives, or [had] two different ways of being. Three is a great number of parents.

Karen: You said you gave Tom a couple of years of the runaround.

Elke: Yeah. I gave him hell.

Karen: You mentioned he was just always there and present, and you knew that. How did that relationship end up growing? What did it grow into?

Elke: Oh, I love that question. It's a really lovely part of my life, actually. So, when I pushed him away, he just stayed, and he was very calm and very patient. I do know that one of my mother's contingencies for getting married was that we were her kids. When my mom and Tom first got married, it was very much a hub and spoke model. My mom was in the middle, and we all had our own relationships with my mother, and everything else kind of bounced off that. So, it took Tom and me a while to get our own connection points. Tom was kind and really steady.

It was the family tradition to go get a Christmas tree together. My mom and sister hated it, so one year, Tom and I decided to go, just the two of us instead. We really started enjoying being together. And we'd been walking for like an hour without even talking. It was kind of like a mini-Christmas vacation for us, getting out of the house, everything seemed to light up in a sunbeam that day. We brought the tree home, and it was so big, and we still talk about it every year. And from then on, there were a lot of things that Tom and I would do, just the two of us.

Whenever I hear of a friend of mine who's marrying into a family and is going to become a stepparent, I always try to give them a pep talk. "This could be the greatest thing ever. Like it's worth the crappy couple of years, or the bad teen attitudes, or whatever, but it's totally worth it. Hang in there." A stepparent and stepchild is a very special relationship. [It was] one of the best of my life.

CHAPTER EIGHT

THE SELF

REFLECTION: 500 THINGS

While we were married, it was common for me to be out of town for a conference at least once a month. David would stay home with the kids, work, and manage the household. On this particular occasion, I had just stepped out of the airport into the February frost, only to find my car buried in snow. Eager to get home, I quickly brushed off the top layer and let the defroster take care of the rest. The kids were four and five years old and seemed to change daily, I didn't want to miss another minute. Five days was a long time to be away from them.

I left the luggage in the car and ran up the stairs to find two giant smiles waiting for me at the front door. A barrage of excited words spilling out.

"Mama! Did you bring us something from your trip?"

"Can you do bedtime books tonight?"

"The cat puked on your bed while you were gone."

And now I also had a giant smile on my face. I chased them into the living room for snuggles and tickles.

"Is your luggage still in the car?" asked David. "I'll run out and get it."

I escorted the kids through our usual bedtime routine (i.e. bath, brush, books, and bed) and quietly shut their bedroom door behind me, nourished from their love. I found David sitting at the kitchen counter when I walked into the living room, and a barrage of words came spilling out of me.

"Funny how the mail doesn't open itself."

"Can you please not leave laundry in the dryer overnight? It just gets stinky."

"It would be a miracle to come home and find a clean kitchen. There is a working dishwasher, ya know."

Sadly, this had become a well-rehearsed script in my head. I was predictably becoming a contemptuous wife, which is just about the worst thing you can do to a marriage.

David stood up and walked over to me, face to face, "It would be a miracle if you came home and saw the 500 things I did do, and not the five I didn't." He turned and walked away.

I stood there a little stunned and really sad. He was right. He was totally right. At that moment, I realized I was building a case against my husband, and against our marriage. I didn't see the 500 things, because I wasn't looking for them. I was looking for a reason, any reason, to write myself out of my marriage.

Like most of us, whatever I went looking for, I was sure to find. What was I looking for?

A parachute.

MAKE A PLAN

I began to see our new reality for what it was. This would be the cadence of our family and my lifestyle. There was an encroaching sense of dread with each transition. Every precious moment that I squeezed with my children meant I was also closer to being alone. I realized I needed a plan, or I'd lose my mind. The silence would swallow me whole, if I stayed in this empty house, drowning in the absence of my children. So, I developed tactics for those first brutal hours after pickup.

I scheduled dinners, walks, hikes, or happy hours with friends, timing them for just after the swap so I wouldn't get caught in the current of self-pity and despair. I made dinner reservations in advance at restaurants too nice for children, places where I could eat a meal while it was still hot and use both hands at the same time. I bought movie tickets ahead of time, choosing films I knew the kids wouldn't enjoy—R-rated dramas or foreign films with subtitles. I eagerly agreed to more and more work opportunities out of town. Interestingly, I didn't feel lonely when I was traveling alone. But being home alone was a different story.

RE-KNOW MYSELF

It is common to lose touch with who we are and what we truly want, when we are enmeshed in a partnership blurring the lines of autonomy. At least that's the model the Western world has been presented with. Marriages and partnerships seem to be a contract of fusion. Sometimes this happens consciously, and other times it's subtle. We might stop playing music loud because our partner gets irritated. Our food choices might change to accommodate their dietary restrictions. Even religious and political beliefs might swing in favor of our partners' preferences. We are all familiar with the need to compromise in a partnership. But sometimes it's not until we are asked to compromise that we realize what we have given up, and what we want to hold on to.

Divorce was very disorienting to my internal compass, and I found myself asking the common midlife crises existential questions: "Who am I?," "What matters to me?," "What do I want to do with my free time?" My life postdivorce looked nothing like it did entering the marriage. I was still pretty footloose and fancy free at 30 when I met David. I spent the better part of my 20s traveling and working seasonal jobs, with a sailor in every port. My passport was well worn. My perspective of the world, and myself, was always expanding. Oh, those were the good old days.

Many things changed over the course of our marriage, with becoming a mother amongst the most significant. The early years with our babies were very demanding and home centric. There was no time or energy for extracurricular activities. I grieved the loss of my freedom and who I had been, while simultaneously rejoicing in the arrival of our sweet healthy babies. This was also a very disorienting time as I reinvented my life as a partner, mother, homemaker, and business owner.

With divorce came the threshold of reinvention again. I suddenly had white space in my life that had previously been gobbled up by partnership and parenthood. Given the choice, I would happily spend my time with my children all day, any day. But that was no longer an option, so I needed to start thinking about how I was going to reorient myself again. It was as if the well-known poet Mary Oliver was standing in my kitchen asking the question, "Tell me, what is it you plan to do with your one wild and precious life?"[1]

DANCING THROUGH DIVORCE

During my first year of being re-singled, I was approached by the director of the professional dance company in town. She was inviting me to join the company for their gala concert. I had grown up in the dance studio, performing and teaching. It was deeply woven into my identity and my joy. Performing with Headwaters Dance Company had been a longtime aspiration of mine but felt completely out of reach at age 40. I hadn't performed in years, nor was I taking regular technique classes, unlike the rest of the company members who were mostly in their twenties. But I agreed to audition and see what my body and brain could muster. As it turned out, I had enough muscle memory and courage to say yes.

With performing comes rehearsal. I knew there would be a massive time commitment, which I welcomed as an antidote to too much free time ruminating in my home alone. However, I now had conditions. I told the director I was unwilling to relinquish time with my kids in exchange for rehearsal. I had just relinquished 50% of my time with them, and I couldn't stomach more loss. I was willing to rehearse during the day when they were in school,

---

[1] Oliver, M. (1990). The summer day. *House of light* (p. 60). Beacon Press.

or nights when they were scheduled with David. I was firm in my conviction to prioritize motherhood.

Fortunately, the director agreed, and I once again came alive in the dance studio. Not only was my body getting in shape, but my brain was also being challenged, and I had a built-in community. This was the gift of the performing arts, and it was a gift to my emotional, social, and psychological health. I managed to survive the physical and mental demands required of me. It wasn't always pretty, but my fellow company members were very patient with my old brain and body. I was proud of the final production and what I had accomplished. This was an essential step in my journey of rediscovery and building a fulfilling life, even when my kids weren't there to fill all the moments with me.

MY NEST

Reclaiming myself also meant reclaiming my space. In our case, I retained the family home which, I came to realize, was filled with marital ghosts. I continued to shift and shuffle furniture around trying to make the space my own. I would pick the economical projects that were in reach for me like changing up the artwork, hanging new curtains, and painting a wall. It was easier to change the visible elements of my home than the invisible residue of a strained marriage.

I tried not to get myself into anything that would require a second set of hands. It became heartbreaking every time I needed someone to hold a ladder, stand back and tell me if the picture was straight, or help move a piece of furniture. I was talking to an empty room, and no one was there to lend a hand. I hated asking for help, so did it sparingly. However, I hated *needing* help even more. It was then that the Power Hour I previously mentioned became my saving grace.

THE DIVORGASMIC ERA

Eventually, I managed to overcome my resistance to pleasure and started to dip my toe into planning travel and adventures. I made my way to Alaska to ride a bike across a frozen lake to the face of a glacier. I sailed with friends on a catamaran through the Bahamas. I floated numerous whitewater rivers and bagged a few peaks. I started filling up my cup of joy. As a result, I became a better parent and a better person. The joy that was filling me up spilled over into all my relationships, including the new ones.

There's a phase in divorce recovery that most of us don't recognize, let alone talk about. I call it *The Divorgasmic Era*. It's that heady, intoxicating, dangerous period where you suddenly remember you're a sexual being with freedom. After years of marital autopilot, where intimacy was often either routine or nonexistent, being back on the dating scene can feel electric. That cute guy or gal you regularly see at the grocery store. They're fair game now. You can flirt with the barista, the store employee, the bike shop assistant, the flight attendant, the nurse, etc. And with shared parenting duties more definitively set, there certainly is time without kids for you to actually go out on dates. Suddenly, divorce has a silver lining, glimmering in the distance.

Although, as a divorce consultant, I have come to believe that anyone who has been divorced less than a year, should have a sign attached to their back:

WARNING—IN DIVORCE RECOVERY. Grief and trauma still unprocessed. Likely going to make dopamine-driven, impulsive decisions, to soothe my wounds and numb my emotions. Prepare to be hurt by my inability to commit or think clearly. PROCEED WITH CAUTION.

As soon as David moved out and long before the divorce was final, we released each other to date freely and openly. When it comes to new relationships, I recommend that all divorcing couples have the *Red Light—Green Light* conversation. Imagine that one partner believes as soon as the word *divorce* is mentioned, it signals a green light to start dating. Whereas the other partner believes there is no green light, until the judge signs the final decree. Each couple needs something different. What matters is talking about it before anyone gets surprised. If you aren't in agreement about the dating starting gate, feelings are going to get hurt and drama is likely to ensue.

On the heels of the divorce, my therapist had been clear with her prescriptive advice: "Eighteen months of dating sobriety, Karen. Not eighteen months of heavy flirting, casual sex, or even situationships. I recommend eighteen months of pure singlehood, and that clock doesn't start until the day you walk out of the courtroom. I suggest you date yourself for a while and see what you discover." I nodded, fully intending to follow her advice. It was the same advice she gave me prior to meeting David, which at the time I also intended to follow. We all know how that turned out.

This time would be different. I recognized the value of "dating myself" so I could recalibrate my identity and desires beyond the lens of being partnered. Singlehood had never been my strong suit. I had pretty much been in a relationship of some kind from ages 17–40. I often felt untethered without a partner and uncomfortable in solitude. I didn't want to repeat the relationship mistakes of my past, so I took her advice to heart. However, intentions and actions do not always align. My divorgasmic parade began almost immediately upon leaving my therapist's office. I was a slow learner.

This new era washed over me one evening, at the grocery store of all places. A man in the produce section caught my eye over the avocados and smiled. It wasn't a polite, neighborly smile—it was a *smile.* Instead of exposing my left hand with a wedding ring that was no longer there, instead of mentally retreating into "taken" mode, I smiled back. My stomach flipped a little. When was the last time it had done anything besides digest stress and harbor anxiety?

I entered into a series of what I came to recognize as *terminal relation-ships*. I knew there was an off-ramp before it even started. I deliberately chose connections with built-in expiration dates, many miles between us, or obvious roadblocks to a long-term relationship. This felt safer than risking real intimacy. It's not like I was going to dive into something serious, but a girl has to eat.

Within about six months of separation, a couple of dear friends took me out to dinner to freshen up my otherwise Eeyore perspective of the world. It was a Mediterranean-inspired tapas menu. The entire restaurant smelled of exotic Middle Eastern spices. It was common for patrons to sit for hours tasting different dishes late into the night. We did as well, recalling old stories and laughing until our cheeks hurt. There was a mini resurrection of myself for those few hours, who was happy, lighthearted, and engaging with the world around me.

Our waiter took note of my radiance and started to chat me up between courses, and there were a lot of courses. I delighted in the attention and drank it up like a desert palm thirsty from years of drought. Divorce had really done a number on my self-esteem. Its overarching theme of rejection and failure had bled into my identity and self-worth. The young waiter provided me with a healing salve to the wounds I walked with daily.

After dinner, we headed to the river to watch the sunset.

"Well, that was fun," I declared, on our walk to the bridge.

"You still got it, McNenny," Chris remarked in his supportive voice. "He was super into you."

"Oh hell, I'm probably 10 years older than him. He was just jockeying for a bigger tip, which he got," I protested.

"I don't know," Clara interjected. "He seemed sincerely interested."

"Yeah, you think so?" I paused and considered my options. I actually had options.

By all means, dive into the dating pool. But first, be clear about who you are and what you are willing and unwilling to accept. It *is* a time of discovery, and I encourage you to embrace the opportunity for reinvention. Not everyone needs an 18-month dating hiatus postdivorce. However, taking time to process your divorce and getting to re-know yourself creates a sturdy foundation for future relationships. Six months to a year of dating sobriety typically works well, provided you're doing the work of processing the divorce emotionally (i.e. the grief, the anger, the confusion—all of it.) Enter your divorgasmic phase emotionally buoyant. Whether you're just looking for temporary flings or deep connections, know your ability to handle the spectrum of relationships before entering them.

In addition, I might also add, trust that while you're figuring out your postdivorce dating life, your ex will be experimenting as well. How you handle their new relationships might speak volumes about how well you can handle your own.

THE GREEN-EYED MONSTER

Of course, David was participating in his own version of the divorgasmic phase and also started dating. Within the first year, I got wind of a more serious girlfriend on the scene. This was new territory for our family. I had a strong and surprising reaction to this news, and I can't quite explain why. I didn't want to be with David, but the green-eyed monster renting out space in my heart didn't want anyone else to be with him either. And I certainly didn't want anyone moving in on my mama territory. I had lots of questions about the "new woman," as I started to dig in the dark corners of the web.

I quickly learned that late-night social media scrolling is a masochistic way of shopping for pain. I wanted to find unflattering photos and information about this woman. I'm not proud of myself. It was incredibly unfair to someone I had never met. But the emotional hijacking that takes place in divorce recovery should not be underestimated. People do and say crazy stuff when they are going through divorce. I wasn't exempt. I didn't expect this new development to sting so much. It was another marker that our love story was indeed over, and the role of the leading lady, previously held by me, just got recast.

Even worse was stumbling onto pictures of your co-parent with their new romantic partner having the time of their lives at the beach, on a hike, or with your old friend group. And the most painful pictures: with your kids. No good will come of these searches, which is why I highly recommend all divorcing couples unfriend and restrict access to each other's social media accounts. When I suggest this to clients, some couples tell me it's really not necessary. However, that's the best time to do it, *before it is necessary*. When it's a mutual agreement completed at the same time, it feels less personal and more practical. Things might change over time, but in the early stages it's a form of protection for your future relationship.

TAP THE BREAKS

Most of us wish to move on and have a new, successful, and loving relationship. I know now (and through personal experience) there's a temptation to start introducing a new relationship early on in the courtship. People tend to be excited, and everything is wonderful because their flaws, and ours, haven't been revealed yet. Both people are typically on their best behavior for the first few months, and each is riding high on the flood of dopamine and oxytocin that comes with a new courtship. The push and pull of early dating literally changes the chemistry of our brains.

If you're dating and you're excited about someone, great. I'm happy for you. Go introduce that person to your friends—*not your kids*. David and I actually put a clause into our parenting plan: *No new romantic partner will be introduced to the kids until the new relationship has been established, and exclusive, for at least six months.* To be clear, this isn't enforceable in a court of law. But it required us both to be thoughtful and talk about new relationships, before one existed. Honoring the agreements we established with each other is part of how we stayed out of court.

When introductions with kiddos do begin, I suggest a slow and safe approach. Starting with a sit-down dinner is probably going to be awkward for everyone. Consider choosing a more casual setting, such as a dog walk, time in the park, or a community festival. Choose an environment where your kids aren't put on the spot and can slip away from the situation, if they need a little space. Keep in mind, you've likely spent months getting to know this person and have already decided you really like them. But for your kids, this is their first date, and it's a blind date. They need time to process and adjust.

It isn't unusual for kids to hold onto the fantasy that their parents might get back together again. This fantasy can bring about complex feelings about the new adults entering their lives. They may not be able to articulate what they are feeling, as it can be a confusing time. The arrival of a new *special friend* is a marker to them that their parents are moving on, and not moving back in together. Essentially, the proverbial other shoe has dropped for them, and they may cycle through grief or anger about the divorce again. In order for this introduction of a newbie to be successful with your kids, it's essential you are thoughtful, intentional, and patient. I must reiterate: how we begin is often how we end.

When a parent introduces a series of short-term emotional relationships, it can cause attachment issues for kids. If a child has people coming and going through their childhood, particularly a new romantic partner, distrust of relationships can often develop. For your kids, it might sound like, "They always leave. No one sticks around. They say one thing and do another."

Later in life, this can show up as either anxious attachment or avoidant attachment styles. An anxious person may obsess about their partner: *Where are they? Why haven't they texted me, are they breaking up with me? Why do people always leave me brokenhearted? I'll just drive by their house and see if they're okay.*

The same child could also lean towards the avoidant style and stay very aloof in their relationships: *Don't smother me. I need my space. I think we are getting too serious. Why get my heart broken, they're going to leave anyway.*

Secure attachment is the healthy balance between these extremes. For many of us, it takes a lifetime to attain (if ever). These are people who have found contentment and reliability with themselves. In the book *Attached*, the authors Levine and Heller clarify, "This balance allows for both closeness and autonomy, creating stable, healthy relationships. Secure attachment is the goal because it supports emotional safety, consistent connection, and resilience in the face of relationship challenges."[2] In short, their moods and needs aren't the sole responsibility of anyone else. Consistent and reliable relationships in childhood can foster secure attachment in adulthood.

It always comes back to the kids and what is best for them. Children need time to process and adjust to the new world of divorce. Roping them into meeting new partners too soon can disrupt their sense of stability and cause confusion. It's a delicate dance, and your kids are only just beginning to learn the steps. Introducing a new partner too abruptly can throw everyone off balance. Timing—even when it feels too drawn out—will pay long-term dividends. If you actually want the new relationship to succeed, go slowly.

THE ONE THAT LASTS

In the wake of my divorgasmic tour de force, I was finally able to settle myself down and start that 18-month clock, again. (The months had to be sequential, I couldn't add up my fits and spurts.) I started to reconnect

---

[2] Levine, A. and Heller, R. S. F. (2010). *Attached: the new science of adult attachment and how it can help you find—and keep—love.* TarcherPerigee.

to my community, and most importantly, to myself. No new relationship could heal my wounds—no one could do that but me. But I was reminded there was something on the other side worth working towards.

Dr. Henry Cloud encourages us to see endings as a way to grow, "Getting to the next level always requires ending something, leaving it behind, and moving on. Growth itself demands that we move on." Moving on from my married identity and emotional entanglement with David seemed insurmountable some days. Esther said to become indifferent. Eventually, I would come to understand what indifference really meant for me and my future.

It wasn't the *absence of emotions*, but rather *the ability to regulate my emotions* in response to David and not react to old triggers. But this would take years to master. I could feel my bandwidth for grace growing; I knew that would be good for our kids and for me. We no longer had to look over our shoulders and ready a defense against the other's criticism. There was greater ease between us, and I started to see the 500 things, not the 5. This wasn't a gift to David as much as it was a gift to myself.

IN THEIR OWN WORDS

The Good Divorce Show
Season 1, Episode 9
Aimee, married 18 years
Daughters 17 and 13 at time of divorce

Listen to the full episode here:

REINVENTING MYSELF

Karen: Knowing what you know now, would you have waited for both of your children to launch and graduate?

Aimee: No, not at all. Because the last five years with my daughters have just been magical. It's been hard for them to go back and forth between two households. Absolutely. But the divorce made us talk so much more about our emotions and relationships than we ever did.

I just remember [that] a typical night at our house would be, I'd come home from work and Matt would have dinner going and offer me a glass of wine. I'd hang out in the kitchen and just talk with him about whatever. And the girls would just be off doing their things. We'd come together for dinner and then we'd all go apart again.

As a mom, I was really dividing my time between my husband who I loved to be with and my kids. Like, sure we were all together, but it really was split up a bit. Coming home … and cooking with my kids and deciding what we wanted to do together—even if it didn't involve cooking: We're going to eat blueberries in front of TV for dinner tonight, or we're going to eat it at midnight. It was so great. Those high school years with them, as a single parent, were wonderful.

Karen: What was going on for you personally?

Aimee: I was clinging to the story that I had told myself was my story. A lot of us … probably relate to that. I do this in many parts of my life. I attach to the outcome, and it's really hard to let go and change paths. I only saw my life as one way, and this did not fall into my story—nor was it my idea.

I am also a bossy person who likes to make choices and guide. I would say I was definitely the leader of our family in many ways. Though we were a very good partnership. I thought, oh my gosh, this is going to destroy our children. We're going to lose our house. Like we're—how—I don't even know. I don't even have a credit card. I don't know how to change the tire. You've cooked dinner for me for the last 20 years. I don't know how to cook. It was ridiculous where my brain went. It was that primitive monkey brain that was telling me I basically wasn't going to survive. And [turned out] it was the opposite.

The other surprising and great part about divorce, I have to say, is my children now have two more adults in their lives who are wonderful, solid humans that they can depend on, because of our village. Yes, I love that my children have advocates. I know they have called on all of us when they've needed different things. It is pretty cool that they have four adults looking out for them. Yes.

Karen: This is a really significant and important paradigm shift, that we move from only seeing the scarcity part of the story, and see all the abundance that can come as a result of what is a really hard decision. But those dark days, they don't last forever, right? It is temporary.

Aimee: Yeah.

Karen: It sucks. Let's be very clear. It's like sitting on the bathroom floor, crying your eyes out, needing all the support in the community to lift us up and out. And it usually takes longer than we want and longer than we think it will, but you do get through it.

Aimee: Somehow you will get through it. It was soul searching and soul crushing. I mean, I don't want to say it like this, but I feel like I was the one who died. I was creating a new me and I [didn't] know who I was anymore without this person always by my side. We were always identified through our couplehood, you know, and I had to create my new self and that does not come easy, but there is a process. It also shouldn't come easy. It shouldn't be like, okay, here I go get a new life. It's a process of just working through the hard stuff.

It's been a while since I thought about those days, Karen. And I didn't want to think about them for a while. Now I think back about them only because it was the process of becoming who I am now. A few weeks ago, my youngest daughter moved out of the house, so I am sitting in an empty house right now for the first time ever in my life.

I am about to be 46, I've never lived alone. You know, wow it's kind of amazing and really valuable. It's really useful to build a relationship with ourselves and to really fall in love with ourselves, before we go out there and start falling in love with other people. But most of us, myself included, skip over that part. I went from living in my family home, to a dorm, to roommates, to Matt my boyfriend, to then marrying him.

I am now living my life as a single woman, making my own decisions, having the means to take care of myself. The first thing I really, truly loved about being divorced was the control of my own schedule. That I could go do things on my own, I could make choices, I could travel, I could work, I could grow, I could think about myself and my needs and desires, and not be split in the way that, you know, I had been for decades.

Karen: That's a huge shift.

Aimee: Yes, huge. And I journaled so much about it. I wrote letters to my former spouse that I never sent. I wrote letters to my kids that I would read, not send. I processed my emotions on paper. I really think that writing it down helped me see patterns. It helped me let go. It helped me grieve and celebrate at the same time. And as I did that, I began to notice who I was without this marriage. And I also noticed that there were things I had been neglecting: dreams, hopes, passions. Things that got pushed aside for the life we were building together that I could now pick up again. And it was like rediscovering myself. Rediscovering my power and my voice and my ability to make decisions without consulting another person.

Karen: That's so powerful. You talk about journaling and soul-searching, and really it's like a toolkit for reinventing yourself.

Aimee: Absolutely. I also took time to experiment. I tried new things. I took art classes. I joined hiking groups. I did things I had always wanted to do but never made time for. And slowly, over months and years, it felt like shedding layers that weren't mine, layers of habits, expectations, roles, and really stepping into the core of who I am. And I can honestly say, Karen, I feel more like me now than I ever did before marriage. And that's not to say I didn't love that life, it's just that I've realized how important it is to be fully known and fully responsible for your own joy.

Karen: And it sounds like journaling was the anchor for that. Did you do anything else along with that, any practices, routines?

Aimee: Yeah, I would say setting intentions. I would write down what I wanted for the day or the week. I started practicing gratitude in very small ways. I began to meditate in the mornings. I started exercising consistently, but not as punishment. I started seeing my body as a partner instead of a tool. And all of those things combined really started to create a structure that supported the new me. And what was amazing, Karen, was how much more confident I became in other areas of my life because I was feeling solid in myself. My relationships, my work, even the small things, just walking into a room with confidence, that really came from all of this inner work.

Karen: You're talking about a total reinvention, really. And you said it wasn't easy, but it was necessary.

Aimee: Necessary, yes. And it's ongoing. I'm still evolving, but I'm aware of it now. And I'm kinder to myself. I celebrate the wins, no matter how small. I also let myself feel the sadness or frustration when it comes. It's okay. It's part of the journey. And I find myself thinking less about the past and more about what I want my future to look like. And there's freedom in that. There's joy in that. And, you know, I think anyone listening who is in the middle of a divorce or thinking about it, I would say invest in yourself. Lean into your grief, your sadness, your anger. Let it flow through you. Journal it, talk to someone, reflect. And know that on the other side, there is a version of yourself that's waiting to emerge that you may not even recognize yet.

Karen: And that's the rainbow on the other side that you were talking about earlier.

Aimee: Yes! Exactly. And I tell people, it's magical. Not every day, not every moment, but it's real. And it's waiting for you. And the more intentional you are about your own life, the sooner you'll get there. And I don't want anyone to feel shame for finding joy in it. Because it can be joyful. You can love your kids, love your ex, and still love yourself and the life you're creating post-divorce.

Karen: That's a really important message. And as we wrap up, would you share what that looks like now in your day-to-day life?

Aimee: Sure. I wake up in a house I love. I make my own breakfast. I choose my work schedule. I take time for friends. I go on trips. I create memories with my kids, who are now young adults, in new ways that I never anticipated. And I feel a sense of peace and power. And, you know, I look at my former spouse and see someone I deeply respect and care about, and yet I'm fully myself. And that's the thing; being fully yourself, after divorce, that's the gift. That's the treasure. And it's worth every tear, every journal entry, every late-night worry. It's worth it.

CHAPTER NINE
THE LOGISTICS

REFLECTION: IN THE BLEACHERS

Anya's jump rope team was preparing to perform at a big event. David and I were squeezed into the bleachers with the other parents, watching the dry run.

"The kids need to be at the Adams Center, in their blue t-shirt, at 5:30 p.m." The coach for the Super Skippers team was getting kids and parents organized for the half-time show for the college basketball game Friday night. "Parents can dump and run at the North parking lot. Coaches will be waiting, ready to wrangle. I want to meet all the parents before you leave, so come get a schedule from me and say hello."

She approached our little cluster of parents, handing out sheets of paper as she went. She conversed easily with the other parents; this monthly routine was nothing new. When she reached us, however, she paused, her face suddenly frozen. She held the schedule awkwardly between David and me.

Her eyes darted back and forth between us, a small furrow appearing between her brows. "Who do I give ..." she started, then stopped herself, sighed, and went for it: "Are you guys divorced? I thought I heard you were, but I can't really tell."

I felt a small surge of triumph. We were changing other people's perception of what divorce could look like, starting with the absence of hostility. "We are divorced," I said with a smile. "We'll take two, one for each home, thank you." Relief flooded her face as she handed each of us a schedule.

I was so proud at that moment. Our hard work was paying off for our family. Our daughter could enjoy her Super Skippers team and not worry one tiny bit about her parents, or what kind of scene they might make. Children are always watching their parents' relationship, married or divorced. How co-parents treat each other will echo through their children and into future relationships.

Kids get to be kids and worry about kid things. Our job was to avoid becoming Anya's pouty, passive-aggressive, prickly, divorced parents. I was grateful we were always respectful of each other in public settings, even when things were spicy between us. We have had plenty of scrappy takedown arguments behind the scenes, but we work hard to keep it together publicly. Which also includes how we talk about each other when we aren't in the same room.

We were finding our groove as a 2Home Family and succeeding.

The new *was becoming the* norm.

IT'S COMPLICATED

I was tucking the kids into bed, where all the juicy conversations take place, and asked my standard monthly question, "How are things going living across two homes?" followed by, "Is there something Daddo and I can do to make your 2Home life more happy?"

"Complicated," came Anya's singular succinct response.

I couldn't agree more. She nailed it. "Tell me more about that."

"Well, sometimes. there is a thing you want, and you look all over and can't find it, and then remember it is at the other house. But most of the time, I just say, oh well, and figure something else out. But sometimes I am sad when I don't have my butterfly wings when I want them."

"Yeah," Dwyer chimed in, "like my blue remote-control car."

"Oh kids, you know you can always tell us if there is something you need. It's easy to run to the other house," I reassured them.

This is why divorced families need systems. Living across two homes *is* complicated, and kids are already complicated enough, so why make it harder on ourselves? One of the first things I hear from clients when they reach out is, "We don't know how to do this." And they're absolutely right, nobody knows how to *get* divorced, let alone how to *be* divorced. Lawyers will help with the former, divorce education will support the latter.

What follows are a series of tools from The Good Guide to support your 2Home magic. If you pay attention to these areas, I predict your divorce will have a higher probability of success. Yes, let's start thinking about successful divorces as the goal. None of us wants to get divorced, but if they are going to keep happening, then we better figure out how to *be* better divorced families, for our kids' sake, for the sake of society, and for our own sake.

THE GOOD GUIDE: COMMUNICATION

I had two parents in my Zoom room for a co-parent counseling session. They had been divorced for several years and things weren't going well, which is why they were talking to me. The first thing I try to do is reorient parents back to the one thing they have in common: how much they love their children. No one understands that love more fully than the other parent. Love is transformative and powerful. Love is the destination.

"To start us off today, I would like each of you to tell me a story about your kiddo from this past week that made you smile."

Both parents listened openheartedly, smiled at each other, and delighted in hearing a happy moment from the other home. I chose to close the session by building a bridge of appreciation between co-parents.

"Before we wrap up today, I would like you to say thanks to your co-parent. Consider something they bring to your kids' life that you don't."

Mom thanked dad for being into video games and wrestling with their sons. Dad was, in turn, grateful that mom kept track of all the birthday party stuff and playdate parent phone numbers.

I reflected back to them, "It's nice to see the two of you talking about your kids together. I know this isn't always easy. How often do you have conversations like this, when you are just sharing stories and talking about what's happening with your boys?"

Their faces went blank, no one spoke, and their eyes started to dart around. Finally, almost simultaneously they replied, "We don't talk. We haven't talked like this for years."

Mom went on to clarify, "We don't really have conversations, it never ends well. All of our communication is on the app, Our Family Wizard."

Now, there's nothing wrong with using Our Family Wizard or similar co-parent apps; they are a very useful tool for some families. But how can we possibly provide wrap-around parenting support for our kids, if we can't talk to our co-parent about what is going on with them? The new crush. The bully on the playground. The struggle in history class. The new interests. Our kids deserve more than: *When is pick-up? You owe me $53. Meet you outside the movie theater. Don't come into my house.*

This couple had traveled through a dumpster fire of a divorce and left as enemies in a pile of ash from which they never recovered. They were off course and waited too long to make a course correction. Please don't let this happen to your family. Communication is the cornerstone of the co-parent relationship. It's the one thing you have to do; talk about your kids so you can raise them cohesively.

PARENT HUDDLE

David and I recognized early on that we needed to arrange offstage time to talk about more than dates and dollars. We needed to have actual conversations to check in about our kids emotional, social, physical, and mental health. Initially, we would connect randomly as things came up. Problem was, I had a lot more things "coming up" than David (I come with a lot of words and worry). He was hitting his communication capacity with me, which was creating frustration for both of us.

We opted for a regular parent huddle one Sunday morning a month, before the kids woke up. We kept a shared Google doc as a rolling agenda, where I placed all my thoughts as they occurred to me. Rather than sending David a message every other day, I could save them all up until our Sunday huddle. Having an agenda also meant there would be no surprises or ambush maneuvers. We would hop on the phone, have a cup of tea, talk about the kids, and work through the agenda. It was a replacement for the moments we used to have when we crawled into bed at night, where we held our debrief about the kids, the day, and the week to come. In the absence of *pillow talk*, this regular huddle kept us on the same page with the kids.

BIFF

Even in the most amicable of divorces there are going to be days your co-parent infuriates you. This is to be expected. Just like in marriage, humans are messy and relationships are complicated. If you feel yourself getting triggered, take a pause before responding in the heat of the moment. You might need to write the angry email and get the big emotions off your chest—just don't send it. Sending messages to a coach or a close friend, before hitting send, can help avoid escalating the situation.

If your relationship tends to be spicy and communication isn't going well, or even if it is, I recommend using the communication strategy called BIFF created by Bill Eddy of the High Conflict Institute.[1] Because BIFF encourages fact-based, problem-solving communication, it makes doing the business of co-parenting (i.e. childcare, scheduling, finances) easier. The intent is to avoid blame, drama, or standoffs and make communication more manageable and less emotionally exhausting.

---

[1] Eddy, W. A. (2019). *Biff: quick responses to high-conflict people, their hostile emails, texts, and social media meltdowns*, 3e. Unhooked Books.

> ## THE GOOD GUIDE: USING BIFF TO COMMUNICATE
>
> **Brief:** Keep responses short, and avoid unnecessary commentary.
>
> **Informative:** Stick to the facts and what needs to be done (e.g. schedules, logistics, children, financial matters), and don't include feelings or place blame.
>
> **Friendly:** Maintain a neutral/courteous tone.
>
> **Firm:** Close the loop clearly, set boundaries, and don't invite more conflict.

BOOMERANG FOLDER

Pretty quickly into the school year, it became clear we needed a system to wrangle all the kids' paperwork: permission slips, artwork, homework, directions for the science project, and so forth. It was information that both houses would need. If David and I were to help each other to succeed, it meant more success for our kids. So, I introduced the *Boomerang Folder*. Just like it sounds, it was a simple folder that contained all the kid-related papers. This folder went back and forth between houses with the kids, like a boomerang.

We didn't send parent notes back and forth in this folder, as that was an offstage activity. But we kept graded papers in there, so kids could share their accomplishments, or struggles, with the other parent when they transitioned. We also tried to divide art projects between the houses, so we could both fill the fridge, showcasing their art. This folder kept both of us in the loop, creating more consistency for the kids and fewer misunderstandings between us.

FAMILY THREADS

During our marriage, it was common practice to send photos of the kids to each other, if one of us was missing out on a special occasion. If I missed a family ski day, David would capture a video of Dwyer mastering a new jump and send it to me in real time. When Dwyer came busting through the door, I could greet him with enthusiasm about his big accomplishment. If David was out of town, I would take photos of Anya's baking extravaganza and pass those along. It felt natural to share these special moments with each other. Why should it be any different in divorce?

Once the kids were old enough to have their own phones, we started a family text thread. This thread became a simple but meaningful way to stitch together their two worlds. When parents show up in the same digital space—laughing, responding, celebrating, and staying informed—it reassures kids that parents can coexist and collaborate. These small acts of sharing help children feel seen by both parents and reduce the pressure they sometimes feel to "catch each parent up" separately. It also sends a powerful message: both parents are plugged in and paying attention, even when schedules or logistics keep us apart.

A family text thread can also be a hub of humor and connection—kids can share a meme, parents can send encouragement, or everyone can laugh at the same inside joke. In addition to the family group chat, I also have a thread with just the two kids, and of course I correspond with each of them separately as well. But as a shared communication tool, the family thread is one I highly recommend; it creates a small but consistent bridge across homes and helps maintain a sense of togetherness that supports the whole family.

THE GOOD GUIDE: RESIDENTIAL SCHEDULE

When it comes to the kid's schedule, custody feels like a hostile word, one that shouldn't be applied to children. This framework establishes children as property, which is a problem. Property connotes value, division, and possession. *Kids should never be negotiated over like property.* This isn't an estate being divided, and kids shouldn't feel like they are the source of conflict. That is a miserable experience for kids.

I prefer to use the language *residential schedule*, which asks, "Where will the kids be residing this week?" Not, "Who has custody of the kids this weekend?" I have emphasized throughout the book that language matters. The current and common language around divorce is divisive. If we can change the language, then we can start to change the story, expectations, and ultimately family outcomes.

David and I agreed early on that the kids would have equal time with both of us. It was never in question. We loved parenting and had respect and trust for each other as parents. This is an area where we usually had alignment and ease. Neither of us wanted to lose time with our kids, but we had to accept this as one of the great sacrifices of divorce. Not only did I divorce David, but it also felt like I was divorcing my kids for half of their childhood. It's an impossible reality to imagine and a heartbreak to live through, especially in the early years.

There are innumerable ways you can divide time. When we first moved into two homes the kids were ages five and seven. We agreed on two nights with Mama and two nights with Daddo, which became our standard cadence for a while. In the early months, we tried not to go more than three or four nights in either home. Young children experience time differently than adults, and five days to a five-year-old can feel like an eternity. And as parents, they seemed to change so much in just a few days. We also wanted shorter stays in each home. Everyone was adjusting to the new normal.

We always posted a color-coded residential calendar where the kids could see it: green days were with Mama, and red days were with Daddo. Because young kids have a distorted sense of time, in the early years we would also remind them the day before a transition was going to happen, so they could emotionally and psychologically prepare for it. As they got older, we still posted a calendar, so they could make plans with their friends. We also knew our family schedule would need to grow and change as they grew and changed.

Here are several residential schedule templates parents can consider when building their residential calendars. Note, they're certainly not the only options. Each family is unique, and their schedule should reflect it. It's best if parents can talk about what they are noticing and then craft a child-centered schedule. Consider this resource an invitation to a conversation; a tool to support decision-making, not a decision made for you.

Schedule name	Pattern: Two week view	How it works	Best for
Alternating Weeks	**Week 1:** Parent A (7 days) **Week 2:** Parent B (7 days)	One full week with each parent—Sunday transition recommended	Older kids, with fewer transition days each month
2-2-3 Rotation	**Week 1:** A (Mon–Tue), B (Wed–Thu) A (Fri–Sun) **Week 2:** B (Mon–Tue), A (Wed–Thu), B (Fri–Sun)	Short stays with rotating weekends	Younger kids who benefit from regular contact with both parents
3-4-4-3 3-3-4-4 4-3-3-4	**Week 1:** A (3 days), B (4 days) **Week 2:** A (4 days), B (3 days) +Variations	Balanced combination of short and long stays	Avoids long separations, but every week might look different

(Continued)

(Continued)

Schedule name	Pattern: Two week view	How it works	Best for
2-2-5-5	**Week 1:** A (Mon–Tue), B (Wed–Thu), A (Fri–Tue) **Week 2:** B (Wed–Thu), A (Fri–Sat), B (Sun–Thu)	Two-day blocks plus long five-day stretches, each week different	Don't need the same schedule each week; parents have erratic work schedules
5-2-5-2	**Week 1:** A (Sun–Thu), B (Fri–Sat) **Week 2:** A (Sun–Thu), B (Fri–Sat)	Predictable weekday schedule	Kids who need the same school routine each week

FLEXIBILITY WINS

We came to learn what a 6-year-old child needs is very different from that of a 16-year-old teenager. While it may seem obvious, I often run into families who have doubled down on their original schedule, without considering ages and stages of their kids. I've also met others who are simply unable to discuss the value of making commonsense changes without the presence of lawyers or a judge.

I recommend parents bring an open mind and be flexible when establishing the family schedule. Rigidity is hard on both kids and parents alike. Kids can be unpredictable, emotional, resistant, or even refuse the schedule being presented (especially older adolescents). Parents might be met with work demands, needs from extended family members, or travel opportunities. It's in everyone's best interest to try and accommodate the unpredictable nature of life.

David and I took a very flexible approach to the cadence of our calendar. There was a set standard, which we would deviate from, as needed. Which happened a lot in our family, because both of us had unpredictable work schedules that regularly required out-of-town travel. We developed an approach that looked more like the manager of the local taco bar making up the monthly staff schedule: we covered all the necessary hours, worked around requests for time off, and gave everyone the same number of shifts. In this story line, I was usually the taco bar manager.

CRAFTING THE CALENDAR

If we were planning the schedule for April, we started the process in February, by sending an email to each other listing the days we had a conflict and couldn't be the overnight residential parent. We did our best to respect each other's privacy. It didn't really matter what the conflict was, we chose to follow a "Don't ask, don't tell policy." I might be headed to Seattle to speak at a conference, but I might also be headed to the Bahamas to roll around in the sand with my new lover. Discretion is useful as you begin to build an autonomous life. Having said that, we also agreed to alert each other during our nonresidential time if we planned to be out of town, out of state, out of country, or out of cell service. If there was an emergency, we needed to know if the other parent was reachable and/or in the vicinity.

Based on our listed conflicts, I would then draft a schedule for April, ensuring an equal distribution of days in each home. I would send the proposed calendar back to David by February 15th, to confirm that it checked out with his schedule. By March 1st, we would have our April calendar set. This became our standard operating procedure for years. If one month was a little unbalanced, we would adjust the following month. I would come to learn the ease in which we adjusted our schedule was a rare divorce gift.

To be clear, the decision about the schedule is primarily the parents' responsibility. Whether it's 50-50 or 70-30, it's the work of the adults to make the schedule and implement it. Kids may have preferences on how the time is split, and particularly as kids age, it can be helpful to check in with a teen to make sure they feel the schedule is working for them. A child (or even a young adult) should *never* be asked which parent they'd rather live with. That is a heavy burden for a child and not their responsibility. Most kids don't want to be the decider.

THE GOOD GUIDE: JOB DESCRIPTIONS

A byproduct of divorce is having to take on the responsibility of managing an entire household and two kids, alone. David and I were both going to have a learning curve. This new reality also forced a reckoning with the patterns we'd created during our marriage. Like many couples, we'd fallen into traditional gender roles. It isn't unusual for one partner to over-function on the homefront, creating learned helplessness for the other party. When you're suddenly responsible for your children 100% of the time during your residency, there's no one to defer to, no one to blame when things go wrong, and no one to back you up.

The typical learning curve I see with clients is when one parent has been less involved with the kids and suddenly needs to master school routines, remember the due dates on permission slips, and track that library day is Tuesday and soccer practice is Thursday. The family-focused partner might need to scramble to understand investment accounts, create their first real budget, and make sure all the bills are paid on time. Both must develop skills they'd previously outsourced to their partner and competencies they never needed to develop.

What strikes me most is how society offers grace for financial learning but little patience for parental learning. When someone admits, "I've never managed investments before," we offer resources, books, and advisors. When a parent—often a father—says, "I don't know the name of my kid's teacher or what day to send the gym shoes," we judge rather than recognize this as a skill gap created by years of specialized roles. Everyone needs time to develop new competencies, whether that's learning to get groceries in the house, pack the lunches, braid hair, pay the bills on time, or balance a budget. Divorce changes everybody's job description. Be empathetic and patient as your co-parent manages their learning curve.

IN THEIR OWN WORDS

The Good Divorce Show
Season 1, Episode 8
Erin & Mitch, married 8 years
Two kids, ages 5 and 3 at time of divorce

Listen to the full episode here:

FOR THE BETTER

Erin: No one goes into marriage wanting or expecting to divorce. For me, it brought up a lot of, "Am I failing? Have we done something wrong? How can we get back on track? Is there a way out of this that isn't divorce? Is there a way that we can figure out how to make it work?"

Karen: Sure, and like many couples, you went to counseling. Please talk a little bit about that decision and that work, and why you say that marital counseling was valuable for your relationship.

Mitch: We both had a very willful attitude towards keeping this marriage going. In many ways, that's admirable. In the end, it was misplaced because we were just holding on, gripping it tight. Part of that decision was saying, hey, we need an outsider to help us out.

We went to marriage counseling and worked with a wonderful woman. It was really lovely. We jumped in and got communication tools and clarity. Along the way, I was sharing this with friends, and I remember talking to a coworker who was cynical. He said, "Marriage counseling never works. Look at the stats, man! You're just going to a divorce. Just rip the Band-Aid off, it's a waste of money."

But it was a great process for me and Erin, because we had thoughtful conversations, not just in the room. I remember our drives back from therapy and the conversations we had at home. We were taking those tools and figuring out what we wanted and what each other needed. They weren't working within this structure of marriage. They weren't working for us individually or as a couple.

I give Erin credit. I think she came to the understanding earlier than I did, and she sometimes waited for me. We had a conversation where we let go of that tight grip we were holding to keep the marriage together, including telling ourselves it was what's best for the kids. We came to a shared understanding that it doesn't work, and that's okay.

We went into our next couples counseling session, and Erin said, "This has been wonderful. Thank you so much. Mitch and I have decided we're getting a divorce." The counselor was crestfallen. She said, "What? This is a shock. I really thought we were on the right track." Erin spent the next 15 or 20 minutes consoling the marriage counselor, telling her she was great at what she does. It's just this marriage wasn't going to work for us.

Karen: Do you remember that moment for yourself, Erin, where there was clarity? Some couples talk about fighting for the marriage. I believe we can also fight for a good divorce. The marriage is ending, but there's a forever relationship.

Erin: At the very end, after we decided to divorce, we had a very emotional but heartfelt conversation. We were so grateful we were going to be in each other's lives. We depended on each other for friendship and support. We were relieved we were going to be co-parenting together. The marriage might be over, but we weren't disappearing from each other's lives. We were in it for the long haul.

We joked that there's no one I'd rather be divorced from. There was this guarantee of still being co-parents and partners in that way.

Karen: You're going to share grandbabies and graduations and soccer games and funerals and weddings. People forget that these decisions cast a long shadow in your lives and your children's lives. I hear your love story. There's a reason you came together and created these beautiful babies, and you don't have to discard the goodness that can still exist in the divorce. For you, that's your co-parenting relationship. Mitch, you've said you have high regard and respect for Erin as a parent.

Mitch: I appreciate that not everyone's in the same boat. It's a dynamic we're lucky to have, and I'm lucky to have.

Karen: It's nice of you to gush on your first wife.

Erin: There's no crime in that. I feel the same way. Mitch and I aligned at the beginning because we both really love our kids. That was a common factor.

I'm grateful that Mitch is my kids' father. He's so involved. There can be a tendency for dads not to be included after divorce, or for resentments to get in the way so parents can't come together. I'm grateful Mitch wants to be as involved as he is. I'm grateful for the support, and I'm grateful for my kids that they have a great dad.

Karen: I had a mentor who said it's important to love your children more than you dislike their other parent. Erin, as you were facing the truth that the marriage was complete, what guiding principles did you lean on?

Erin: One thing Mitch and I were clear about was that we did not want a contentious divorce. We are both children of divorce. We had seen it in our families and with friends, and how hard it is on kids.

Every decision came down to the kids and what was best for them. Once that was the focus, things became clear and easy. That was a unifying, clarifying factor.

Karen: Was that an easy place for you to arrive at, Mitch?

Mitch: Yeah. It set the tone for how we went about it. We got a mediator and trusted that collaborative process. Keeping the kids in focus made it clear what was healthy for them.

Erin: We really confused our mediator, too, because during mediation we had inside jokes and laughter. We felt like we were collaborative enough and shared enough values where we could trust that process rather than a more litigious approach.

Once we got through the initial adjustment, we switched into a different co-parent mode. But we were still ourselves.

Karen: Tell me about the decisions you made: The house, assets, logistics.

Erin: We had a family home. Mitch let me and the kids live there until it was the right time to sell. That gave the kids consistency. We were able to bring a spirit of give and take to the process.

We didn't have many finances to split. We wanted the mediator to tell us what was fair under California law. With custody, we started with me having the kids four days a week and Mitch three. The kids were three and five years old, and we felt they should be around their mom a bit more. In the summer, we flipped the schedule to help everyone.

Later, Mitch wanted 50-50 custody. That's where I felt like, okay, I need to be generous. That was really hard. It was heartbreaking not to have them every other week when they were so little.

Karen: Mitch, what do you remember about wanting to shift the schedule?

Mitch: Some things are black and white. Other things are works in progress. What sounds good on paper doesn't always work. Having all weekends off sounds delightful, but then I don't get to take my kids on trips or hikes.

Erin: Different things are better for kids at different times. When they were younger, seeing each of us more frequently was better. A full week away would have been confusing. As they got older, switching less often made more sense. Switching every few days was disruptive.

Agreeing to 50-50 [custody] was hard, but it was best for them. It's best to have a father who's fully present, not a weekend dad.

Karen: I tell parents to write the parenting plan, tuck it away, and liberate your life on behalf of your children. Be flexible. We are the authors of our family story.

Erin: We trust each other as co-parents. We're flexible because we know the other person will reciprocate. Mitch travels for work, I travel too. We give and take. It's easier to be generous when you know it goes both ways. It's better for everyone to not have conflict every time a schedule change comes up. There's a lot of stuff that's beyond our control. And it's better than conflict every time something changes.

Karen: Yes, behavior is contagious. So, for those out there listening and thinking my partner's never flexible, well, if you bring it, then they'll start to trust it, and it starts to become a reciprocal relationship. When you bring flexibility, trust grows, and it becomes reciprocal.

The good divorce doesn't mean it's all easy. There are still struggles of co-parenting and being in a relationship with someone. I remind people it's never too late to have a good divorce. Maybe you're further down the divorce road than Erin and Mitch.

Did you hear something in this episode that you can still apply to your own life? What nugget of wisdom would each of you share?

Erin: Hearing us talk about all of this out loud, I feel really proud of both of us for how we handled it. If there's anything I've taken away, the most meaningful thing, it really comes down to the kids and prioritizing them. Prioritizing them in a way that made our actions fair made anything that needed to happen straightforward.

Karen: Beautiful. How about you, Mitch?

Mitch: Your family and your joy can look a lot different than what you think it might look like. And it's yours to make.

Karen: The story is ours to write, and you can continue to foster a beautiful family story.

CHAPTER TEN

THE NEW

REFLECTION: FAMILY TIES

Four years into the renovated version of our family, Anya's first middle-school choir concert was no longer an event for which we had to brace ourselves. We knew what to expect. My parents would arrive at the gym ridiculously early, to satisfy my mom's anxiety about getting good seats. She and my dad would save an entire row in the bleachers for David and his dad, myself, Dwyer, and my sister's family. We didn't question if we would all sit together, that was a given. Anya didn't have to dart her eyes around the crowded bleachers searching for a divided family, she could easily find her family, together.

Per usual, Dwyer would sit between David and me. As the kids walked single file through the gym and up onto the bleachers, we were all nudging each other, pointing towards Anya in the lineup.

"There she is, Dwyer, on the top riser," David whispered, pointing out his big sister.

"Oh yeah—wow, she looks so pretty," came the admiration from her little brother.

"Yes, she is. She gets that from her Mama," came David's reply, without looking in my direction. He just kept smiling at Anya.

I'm sure I had an expression of shock on my face, as the comment washed over me. I couldn't remember the last time David had overtly said something kind to me, or about me. Not that we were overtly rude or hostile to each other, but warmth and kindness hadn't really made its way back into the vernacular. My entire heart softened towards this man, the father of my children, my once-upon-a-time husband and all-too-often adversary. A tectonic shift took place in that moment; the slightest notion of kindness can have a powerful effect.

I leaned into Dwyer and whispered in his ear, but loud enough for David to hear, "Yes, but her musical talents, she gets that from Daddo."

As we worked to sew our family back together, I was reminded that our kids had, and always would be, a tapestry created from both of us. Why would anyone intentionally try to tear that apart?

THE NEW WOMAN

In late spring, David approached me at Dwyer's T-ball game, "So, I have been seeing someone for quite a while now, more than six months, and I'd like to introduce the kids." Hearing this news ignited my nervous system and I was flooded with anxiety. "She would like to meet you before she meets the kids. So, you're probably going to get an email from her." He turned and walked away.

Two days later, an unfamiliar email popped up in my inbox. The subject line read: "Hi from David's Friend."

My stomach tightened and my breath stopped short in my lungs. I spun through all the predictable questions racing through my head.

We had found our family groove; there was more familiarity and routine for the kids. A new partner on the scene felt like the greatest threat of all right now.

My finger hovered over the mouse. I clicked open.

The email went like this:

Hi Karen!

Hope you don't mind me emailing you. I would love to get together and meet. Maybe we could go have a cup of tea? I think it's really important for you to meet me and get to know me a bit, before I spend any time with your kids. It's so important to keep it comfortable and smooth for Dwyer and Anya, and I think we can facilitate that by getting to know each other. Kids are number one, with no exceptions, in my opinion. So, let me know what you think. I work from home and have tons of flexibility in my schedule. I do have jury duty scheduled for Thursday … maybe some time on Friday?

I look forward to meeting you, Karen. Though I don't know Anya and Dwyer yet, from what David tells me, they are wonderful! You guys are great parents … I know that. They are very lucky kids, and you, very lucky parents.

What the hell was I supposed to do with this? I had been ready to go to battle, and then after reading her email, I wanted to weep. After some quick google-stalking, I discovered she is a Marriage & Family Therapist. Which explains her capacity and wisdom to send me such a breathtaking, kind, and considerate message.

I was cautiously optimistic about having a cup of tea with my ex-husband's new girlfriend. Why did this feel so weird and so right at the same time? It wasn't jealousy; I didn't want to be David's partner. It wasn't disdain; I didn't even know this woman. It was fear. Fear of her presence in our family and how that could pull my kids away from me. But she didn't come to fight or lay claim to any of our family territory. She came in peace—exactly what I'd been wanting, I just didn't expect it to come in this package.

We decided to meet for lunch. She arrived with her hair pulled back in a baseball cap, clad in her understated running attire. I was between clients and dressed professionally for the day. She arrived as a fully actualized woman who didn't need to prove anything to me, or mark her territory, or spread her feathers. She really just wanted to meet the mother of the children of her new boyfriend, before she met the children. This wasn't what I expected, and I adored her for it.

She *got it*. She recognized David, the kids, and I were a family. I wasn't going anywhere. She really cared about David and wanted things to go well for them, which meant she needed things to go well with me. Before long, she was in the bleachers with us. We found the peaceful path to rise above pettiness and a territorial struggle, and in return we all got to delight in the joy of the kids.

Blended families ask us to stretch. Not just logistically, but emotionally. They challenge old ideas of loyalty and boundaries, and invite something more nuanced: generosity, curiosity, and humility. My lunch with her could've been strained, performative, or avoided altogether. But instead, it was … nice. We showed up as mothers first, not competitors. No need to posture or protect. We both understood that the relationship we built would shape the kids' perceptions of love and family. It was a simple lunch, but the implications would ripple throughout our family for years to come.

LOVE IS A RECIPE

As we headed into the school year, the new woman was around more: attending activities, giving gifts to the kids, and helping out at David's house in the mornings when he had an early morning work shift. She would head to his place early and feed the kids breakfast and walk them to school. It is hard enough to lose time with your kids, but when that time is then appropriated by a new mother figure, it stings, no matter how lovely the woman is.

One Thursday morning, Dwyer needed his recorder for music class, and it had been left sitting on the piano at my house, not an uncommon occurrence for 2Home Families. Fortunately, we lived close to each other, and the kids' elementary school was located between our homes. I grabbed the recorder and told her I would see them on the playground. I relished any opportunity to get bonus time with the kids.

I was ahead of schedule, so I passed the school and started walking down David's street. I could see the kids in the distance, having just stepped outside, headed my way, "Morning, everyone!" I called out.

"Momma!" called out Dwyer. Together, with his sister, they ran into my arms. A cinematic moment every divorced parent dreams of. The four of us walked together, the kids bouncing between the two of us. She had a natural ease with them that I appreciated—not trying too hard, just being present and engaged. After hugs and reminders about after-school pickup, the kids disappeared into the school.

The new woman and I chatted for a few minutes about the excitement of the new school year. Then she paused, seeming to consider her words carefully.

"Your kids are beautiful, and they're so protective of you. It's very clear they love you deeply. They often talk about you and tell me how wonderful you are. They are very loyal to you, Karen."

The words hung in the air between us. Coming from someone else, it might have sounded like flattery or manipulation. But I could tell she was being thoughtful and sensitive—her background as a Family Therapist showing through in how she approached this delicate topic. She didn't say it outright, but I picked up on the deeper implication: my children didn't want to betray their love to me and might be holding back emotionally.

"They talk about me a lot?" I asked, a little surprised. I talked about my children all the time—I guess I hadn't considered my children going on about me.

"Anya especially," she said with a gentle smile. "She'll start a story about something fun we're doing, then pivot to 'My mom makes the best pancakes' or 'My mom would love this song.' It's sweet."

My children were loyal little souls, and in their minds, there was only so much love to go around. If they gave some to this new woman, did that mean taking it away from me? They were protecting my feelings, guarding their affections like finite resources.

I find it so humbling: I was worried about new siblings making my kids feel threatened, while they were worried new adults would make me feel threatened. I started to realize we were all worrying about invisible shadow figures. That evening, as I tucked Anya and Dwyer into bed, I thought about how to broach the subject. After our usual bedtime stories in the green chair, I tucked them in and then sat quietly, holding space for their thoughts to bubble up.

I was the one who spoke first that night, searching for the right words, "Daddo's new friend seems nice. Do you like her?" I wasn't trying to investigate; I was trying to open up the topic.

Anya was guarded in her response, "Yeah, she's nice enough."

"Daddo was laughing so hard the other night when she came over to BBQ hamburgers with us, and it was so fun. Daddo was so happy." Dwyer didn't have the filter to hold back on my behalf, nor should he have to. It is hard to hear about David's happiness, not because I wish him unhappiness, it just breaks my heart to once again be reminded of the painful truth, that we couldn't find that happiness together.

"Well, that's great, I'm happy for Daddo," came my onstage voice, "I also want you to know that you can fully welcome her into your hearts. It's okay. Because remember what we talked about before, if our family grows?"

The kids jumped in together, "Everyone gets their own love pie."

"That's right. Liking her doesn't take away from how much you love me. I get to keep all the love pie you make for me."

Dwyer scrunched up his face, thinking. "So, she gets her own love pie too?"

"If you want to bake one up for her, yes," I said carefully. "And here's the important part—I want you both to know that it's okay to like her. It's okay to have fun with her, to care about her, to be happy for Daddo and her. That doesn't change our love, and it doesn't hurt my feelings."

My heart squeezed. These beautiful children, trying so hard to protect everyone's feelings, carried burdens that weren't theirs to bear. "Really,"

I assured them. "In fact, it makes me happy to know there are more good people in your life who care about you. What could be wrong with more love?"

It struck me then how much we all need conspirators in the quest for love and happiness. We have to help each other get there, even if it's your first husband's new girlfriend. Especially then, because our children are watching, learning what it means to be generous with our hearts, to choose abundance over scarcity, to believe that love isn't a pie that gets smaller with each slice, but a recipe that makes more pie with every person we invite to the family table.

A GOOD DIVORCE INDUSTRY

Since the time of my divorce, now 14 years ago, and more explicitly during the writing of this book, I have spoken to many friends, professionals, and other divorcing families about my grave concerns with the divorce industrial complex. Really, I spoke to just about anyone who would listen. In part, this is why I launched my podcast, *The Good Divorce Show*. My intent has been to invite guests on the show who've had positive divorce experiences that weren't laced with conflict, destruction, and despair. Through the art of storytelling, I want others to hear and believe that a good divorce is possible.

Sadly, I have found this to be a radical and pioneering effort. As I've extolled throughout this book, the divorce industry in America isn't looking out for the best interests of the families and individuals going through divorce. Instead, it serves lawyers and other institutions that financially benefit from divorce. It is an industry financially incentivized by conflict, not cooperation.

Lawyers are doing exactly what they are trained to do: fight for their clients. But in the case of family law, it means pitting parents against each other. It takes two people at their most vulnerable—emotionally raw, financially uncertain, worried about their children—and places them in an adversarial arena. The language itself is combative: plaintiff versus defendant, winning custody, fighting for assets. We've built a system that turns the end of a marriage into a war, then we wonder why divorced couples can't co-parent peacefully and why kids suffer.

The divorce industry resists good divorces, because good divorces aren't financially exploitative. A couple who agrees on terms and files uncontested paperwork might spend a few thousand dollars. A couple locked in bitter litigation can easily spend tens of thousands, sometimes hundreds of thousands of dollars, over the course of years. The system is designed to escalate conflict, not resolve it.

What we need is a fundamental shift in how we approach the end of marriages. Instead of divorce lawyers, we need more divorce coaches, counselors, and consultants. Instead of courtroom battles, we need mediation rooms. Instead of judges making decisions about families they've never met, we need parents making decisions about their own children with professional support and guidance. Families need to design their divorce rather than accept divorce by default.

As I reflect on the hardest of days, like the night the kids were splashing in the bathtub and the best version of myself was nowhere to be found, it became clear I needed to leave *for* my children. It also occurred to me that I should leave while there is still love. Not romantic love, perhaps, but the basic human caring that comes from sharing years of your life with someone. What if we recognized when a marriage had run its course, before it curdled into resentment and anger? What if we could say, "Our marriage isn't working anymore, what can we do to save our family?" Maybe under these conditions, we could find an elegant exit.

The current divorce industry makes this nearly impossible. By the time most couples navigate the legal system, any remaining goodwill has been destroyed. The process itself creates animosity where none might have existed. It forces people to list grievances, document failures, and prove fault. It turns former partners and parents into enemies, to the detriment of the children.

PEACE IS A CHOICE

My story—our story—proves that divorce can be done differently. One family finding a better way might not seem like much against an entire industry, but every revolution starts with someone saying, "There has to be a better way." If enough of us rail against the powers that be, eventually they become less powerful. I believe in a future where, rather than families supporting the divorce industry, the divorce industry supports families. A future where a good divorce is so normal, that we no longer need the word *good* as a descriptor, where it's a given.

When I talk about a good divorce, I'm really talking about allowing our relationships to transform rather than disintegrate. A marriage might end, but the co-parenting relationship continues. The romantic partnership dissolves, but the shared history remains. We need a divorce pathway that supports, rather than suffocates, this transformation. We need help restructuring the family, not tearing it down. It's possible; I've done it, and I've helped other families do it too.

May our relationships, when complete, rest in peace. Not in the bitter, angry peace of exhausted combatants, but in the gentle peace of grief and eventually acceptance. The peace that comes from saying, "We tried, we loved, we created something beautiful together, and now it's going to evolve into something new." This new kind of peace allows family memories to still be created, and for children to know they are loved by both parents, even if those parents no longer love each other. This is the peace the divorce industry could help us find. But for now, we must find it for ourselves.

LATE NIGHT NACHOS

The kitchen clock in my home showed 9:37 p.m., way past bedtime. But the kids just finished their first week of school, Anya in third grade, Dwyer in first grade, and they were celebrating. We had also made it through the first year of "firsts" as a 2Home Family. I was having my own inner celebration, knowing we made it and trusting each day would continue to get easier.

The kids and I had built a ginormous fort in the living room, using every possible couch cushion and blanket we could find. Their favorite Bill Harley CD was playing loud, and the dance party had begun. Occasionally, Dwyer would bound over to the piano and bang out a few notes, adding to the musical cacophony. Anya appeared from the bedroom dressed in an oversized flouncy dress and an arm full of dress-up clothes.

"Mama, put on this big hat and the feather boa. Dwyer, here's your favorite hard hat and a pair of cowboy boots." The dancing continued, as did the laughter.

"Mama, I'm hungry, can we have a snack in the fort?" asked Dwyer, always pushing for one more snack before bedtime.

"Oh yeah, can we make nachos?" chimed in Anya.

To be clear, nachos in my home means chips on a plate, covered in pre-shredded cheese, and then microwaved to perfection.

"Sure, let's make nachos!" I was having so much fun with my kids, felt so lighthearted, I also didn't want the night to end.

I scooped them both up off the ground and plopped them on the kitchen counter. Music continued in the background as they sang along with Bill Harley, "Zanzibar, oh Zanzibar, Zanzibar is very far, you can't get there in a car."

"More cheese Mama," commanded Anya.

With a sufficient pile of cheese perfectly placed on the plate I slid the nachos into the microwave and closed the door. As the plate whirled around, so did the singing, "In Zanzibar, they grow tea, far away across the sea, off the coast of Afri-cee."

We were deep in a fit of giggles when the microwave dinged. The cheese had melted into golden pools; I was coming down from a laughing fit when I took the plate and set it on a hot pad on the counter between Dwyer and Anya. "Be careful, little chickens."

"Mama," Anya caught my attention, and I turned to look at her glowing face. She placed her little sticky hands on both of my cheeks and squeezed my smile, exclaiming, "You're so happy!" Anya burst out, her whole face lit up with a smile that seemed too big for her face, "I love it when you are sooooo so happy."

Her words were like a wall of warm wind that hits when you round a street corner. My children were watching. I thought I was the one looking out for them, but they were just as attuned to how I was feeling. It made my heart hurt to think of all the times I pretended I was fine. They probably knew I wasn't.

"Yes, sweet girl," I said through glistening eyes. "I *am* happy."

Dwyer leaned forward and smacked a kiss on my cheek.

"Me too," he said, pulling back.

"Me three," Anya added, reaching for another chip.

EPILOGUE

THE DIVORCE ECHO (14 YEARS POSTDIVORCE)

I wasn't expecting the echo. We were no longer dissolving our marriage; it was now time to dissolve our divorce, and at the very least, to redefine our relationship. There was a reverberation of familiar feelings: loss, sadness, and disorientation. It wasn't as strong as when we divorced, but still present. I suddenly realized that my co-parent relationship with David was about to change again.

Our children were now 19 and 21, which meant the legal parenting plan no longer applied. They're both young adults, off to college and living on their own. All that to say, David and I don't have much contact anymore. Unless a kid situation necessitates it, which is the only kind of contact we ever have, the necessary kind. It's not like we grab coffee together.

David and I had been in contact almost every week for the last 23 years. The kids had been the tether between us through most of it. As they become more independent, our connection fades, which is to be expected. I just didn't expect the melancholy that would come with it. It's as if we were getting divorced all over again. I realized that I appreciate the familiar presence of David in my life, and I will miss that. I will miss him.

Becoming an empty nester, while single, brought back the phantom pain. This is the time when parents start to plan their own adventures together, without the kids. They lean on each other and help fill the void left by the kids launching. They are comforted knowing they won't be alone as they age; they will have the support of one another. There's a future to look forward to and a new chapter to write together. The absence of a partner, and the absence of my kids, feels like one more poke at an old wound that's not quite scarred over.

I was sharing my thoughts about the divorce echo while on a dog walk with a girlfriend. "I was having another grief-relief cocktail, just like when we got divorced," I clarified to her. "It's like we are now getting a divorce from our divorce."

It was a thought I'd been revisiting. Maybe there's an even kinder and gentler world for us to inhabit as co-parents now. We no longer have to do the really hard day-to-day work of co-parenting across two homes. Now we can bask in the joy and pride we have for our children, as we watch their lives unfold.

"His presence mostly comforts me; my indifference helps with that. I love him as the father of our children; that is one of his gifts. He is the only other person on the planet that can fully appreciate and understand the love I have for those two humans."

"Okay, hold up." Sarah had stopped walking and turned to face me. Her expression was the particular mix of affection and skepticism she reserved for when I was getting a little too heady. "I love you, but you are starting to sound a little like a good divorce evangelical preacher, and you definitely have some magical thinking going on here."

My face said, "What do you mean?"

Sarah continued on without prompting. "You keep talking about your 'good divorce' like it's this mutual transformation you and David went through together." She put a hand on my shoulder. "Karen, how would David describe *his* divorce?"

Valid question. I had no idea what story was playing in his head.

"Just because you've had a good divorce," Sarah continued, "doesn't mean he has."

She wasn't wrong.

When I say a *good divorce*, I mean you can have a divorce that doesn't cost you a fortune, drag on for several years, or pit spouses and kids against one another. A good divorce brings you to a state of indifference and acceptance. Some people can never get there. There are plenty of stories about divorced partners who still can't stand to be in the same room together. That breaks my heart and seems so avoidable. Such a waste of love.

Divorce creates an opportunity for couples who turn out to be poorly matched, to do something proactive to improve the relationship, not make it worse. Sometimes, they were poorly matched from the start—two people who fell in love with the idea of each other, rather than the reality. Sometimes, they grew into different people over the years; their paths diverging so gradually that they didn't notice until they were miles apart. David and I were probably a combination of both.

I had to let go of the idea that a good divorce meant we were both skipping off into our respective sunsets, equally pleased with how things turned out. Life doesn't offer that kind of symmetry. What I could claim was my own experience: my good divorce, my happiness, and my journey toward something better. I didn't need David's experience to validate mine. I was perfectly capable of having a good divorce all on my own, his involvement was not required. I couldn't control his journey any more than I could control the river that runs through town.

Love stories are still love stories, even when they end. The years David and I spent together weren't erased by divorce. The memories made, the children we created, the home we built—all of it happened, and all of it mattered. The ending doesn't negate the value of the story that came before it.

A good divorce, I'm learning, is like a good life—you can only live your own.

APPENDIX

UNDERSTANDING DEVELOPMENTAL STAGES FOR CHILDREN IN DIVORCE AND SEPARATION[1]

---

[1] Used with permission from Parent Team.

AGES 0–2 INFANTS

Comprehension

Infants do not understand divorce on a cognitive level but can sense changes in their environment, such as parental stress or shifts in routine.

Needs

Require consistency in care, a calm environment, and responsiveness to their emotional and physical needs. Frequency in seeing caregivers, along with quality not quantity, is prioritized.

Focus

- Consistent, frequent contact with caregivers
- Attention to attachment needs by both parents (i.e. feeding, diapering, sleep hygiene, etc.)

AGES 2–4 TODDLERS

Comprehension

Toddlers will notice a parent's absence and may express confusion, anger, or fear. Increased clinginess and regression (e.g. bedwetting or tantrums) may occur.

Needs

Clear, simple explanations ("Mommy and Daddy will live in different homes and love you very much") and reassurance through consistent, predictable routines and structures are needed.

Focus

- Consistent, frequent contact with caregivers
- Predictability; visual, color-coded calendars; clarity around schedule; maintenance of relationships

AGES 4–6 PRESCHOOLERS

Comprehension

Preschoolers may see divorce as their fault due to their egocentric thinking. They may not understand permanence and could expect parents to reconcile or fear a parent leaving for the night means they are leaving forever. They may experience fear of abandonment, nightmares, or difficulty expressing their emotions.

Needs

Consistency in care, reassurance of love and care, and validation of their feelings is required, along with consistency and predictability in schedules and routines.

Focus

- Consistent, frequent contact with caregivers
- Reassurance that divorce is not their fault, that they will see both of their parents, and that the adults will figure out the details

AGES 7–11 SCHOOL-AGED CHILDREN

Comprehension

They may have a better understanding of divorce but may see it in black-and-white terms, assigning blame. They may feel torn between their parents. They may experience anxiety, sadness, or anger. They may struggle academically or socially. Those with stronger moral compass—may experience loyalty conflicts.

Needs

They require honest, clear, age-appropriate communication; encouragement to express feelings; and reassurance that the divorce isn't their fault and that they can love both their parents how they choose to.

Focus

- Consistent, predictable contact with caregivers
- Reassurance of love, support, and validation of feelings
- Limitation on adult relationship details

AGES 12–18 ADOLESCENCE

Comprehension

Adolescents understand the complexities of divorce and may experience strong emotional reactions, such as anger, sadness, or embarrassment. They may take sides or feel pressure to support a parent emotionally. They may experience acting out, withdrawal, or taking on adult responsibilities prematurely.

Needs

They require open dialogue (not including adult content or complexity) and validation of their feelings, maintenance of their peer relationships, and encouragement to express their needs without feeling responsible for parental emotions. Consistent schedules are also key.

Focus

- Maintenance of peer relationships
- Reassurance that they are not responsible for their parents' feelings or the adult divorce details
- Comprehension that they have a voice, but not a vote, in the process

AGES 19+ ADULT CHILDREN

Comprehension

Adult children crave a coherent narrative of why the divorce happened. Unlike younger children, they are more capable of handling nuanced explanations. However, they still need to be insulated from the burdening details, like personal grievances or intimate marital issues, yet require enough context to help them understand the situation.

Needs

They require reassurance of family bonds, in addition to freedom from taking sides, validation of their emotions, and clarity that their role is still parent-child (not a mediator or counselor for parents). They also require space to grieve the loss stemming from their parents' divorce. Focus should be on them, and not on the other parent when both parents are present.

Focus

- Mature conversations that insulate adult children from parental divorce details, which can burden their relationship with one or both parents
- Reassurance of love, support, and validation of feelings and family identity
- Continual ensurance that they're kept "out of the middle," especially when planning family events such as graduations, weddings, celebrations, births, and so on

ACKNOWLEDGMENTS

My mom is the sort of lady that stays to the very end of the movie and watches all the credits, willingly. She wants to acknowledge all the people who contributed to the project. On the way out of the theater, she shakes her head in wonder and whispers to herself, "I just can't believe how many people it takes."

So, thanks for being like my mom and staying to the very end to honor the many people who supported me and contributed to this book.

Thanks Mom, for always honoring the creative person inside of me. Every dance class, voice lesson, piano lesson, and performance—all of it was fertilizer for this moment.

Thanks Dad, for being my first and most discerning editor. You nourished my love of words and believed there was a book inside of me.

In 2022, Tacy Trump (no relation) with *Voice America* reached out to see if I wanted to produce a podcast about company culture and leadership. My response was a clear and resounding, "No thanks. But can I do a podcast about divorce, and call it *The Good Divorce Show*?" Thank you for being my media-midwife Tacy, you got this ball rolling.

In 2024, Andy Earl with *Write it Great* reached out and asked if I had ever thought about writing a book about divorce? My response was a clear and enthusiastic, "Yes, for about 15 years." So grateful to Virginia Combs,

Bee Avila, Corrine Hickin, and the rest of the *WIG* team for helping me find my words. I simply could not have done this without you.

Thanks to the outstanding team at Jossey-Bass and Wiley Press, who gave this book the oxygen and platform it needed to come to life. Amy Fandrei, you made the leap of faith to bet on this unknown, unproven, but highly enthusiastic horse. I am forever grateful for your courage. Special thanks to Sophie Thompson and Moses Ashirvad for being my personal compass and keeping all the moving pieces on schedule. Just when I thought I had crossed all my Ts, and dotted all my Is, along comes Jan Neal to master the small and critical details.

A book is only as good as its developmental editor; lucky for me I had Sunnye Collins walking alongside me. You were willing to let me excavate until the literal 11th hour, to find what this book needed to be. Your patience and insights were such a gift.

Jen Schimbeno and Brandyn Roark Caires, Parent Team Founders, you appeared at the moment I needed you most. Not only were you generous with your contributions to the book, but you have been a buoy in my professional life. It is a joy disrupting the divorce industry with you.

Where would an artist be without the valuable patrons who encourage, support, and fund the vision of the artist? Traci Sylte, you were that first patron and essential cheerleader who believed in me, before I believed in myself. Thanks also to Pat and Karen McNenny (the other one), Kathleen McNenny, Rob Stepans, Kathy Witkowsky and Jay Kirby, Sally Jo Beck, Lynn Compton, Kara McMahon, and Lizzi Judda, all of whom offered an important boost in this process.

Thanks to my fellow word lovers and dear friends, Kadi Cole, Jeni Fleming, Chad Harder, Kerri Hiatt, Mercedes Barker, and Andrew Knox, who got me through the existential crisis of writing a book, by reading messy first drafts, listening to the first readings, providing valuable feedback, and encouraging me to keep going. Thanks to Laura Munson and all my Haven Sisters—Sarah Hunter, Lila Bahin, Judith Scimone,

Stefanie Williams, Sarah Levin, and Jodi Wolf. Thanks to Eric Anderson for offering the most nourishing woodland writing retreat a girl could ask for. Thanks to my neighborhood sister-wives Ruth Ritter, Nancy Hobbins, Carla Squires, Molly Bradford, Eden Atwood, MC Jenni, Joy French, Heather Adams, and Elke Govertson, for keeping me and the kids upright through my divorce recovery.

My classroom for this book has been with my clients, and guests on the podcast. Without you, I would know nothing. Your perseverance inspires, your struggles instruct, and your hope for something better gives me the momentum to keep learning. Thank you for trusting me with your precious lives and stories.

There is not enough gratitude for my right arm, brains, backbone, cheerleader, systems builder, and duct tape, Kate "The Great" Liles. You have been my Miracle Grow.

My deepest appreciation goes to my extraordinary children who have been my most valuable instructors in this messy and blessed journey of life. You didn't sign up to be a part of this living laboratory called divorce, and yet you have always brought the best version of yourself to the story. Thank you for your love and encouragement—to the moon and back.

And just like going to the movies, if you stay through the end of the credits, you get a bonus scene. Enjoy!

A CHRISTMAS BONUS

The holidays loomed ahead like mountains on the horizon—beautiful from a distance but daunting to climb. Every divorced family I knew had horror stories about holiday warfare: kids shuttled between houses on Christmas Day, Thanksgiving dinners eaten in shifts, the magic of the season crushed under custody agreements and resentment. David and I were determined to do it differently. We wanted our children's holiday memories to be filled with joy and family togetherness, not fights over who got which hours on which days.

"Who *gets* Christmas" sounds more like a land grab and less like a family holiday. Nobody wants to miss out on Christmas. What did that even mean? *Does it start with Christmas Eve? The whole next day? The entire school break? Where would Santa deliver gifts? Was I going to miss out on Christmas morning magic? Would we buy presents together? Will we be required to split Christmas down the middle and insist our kids get out of their new cozy Christmas PJs to pack up and relocate?*

We quickly agreed that "splitting" Christmas like a holiday fruitcake was not going to work for our family. We both wanted to be present for the Santa moments. Our kids were little and there was a lot of magic to be had, and they wanted to share it with both of us. So, that's what we designed: a hybrid holiday.

I would be the holiday host our first year. This meant Christmas magic would happen in my home but just not for me alone. David and I worked to find a way to share Christmas morning that would set us up for success. This was our first Christmas, just 60 days into separated life, the pain was still raw and sensitive. Being tender towards each other wasn't always our go-to response when we were together. But if the kids were in the room, we had greater restraint. So, we talked it out and devised a plan, ahead of time, that worked for our family.

With Thanksgiving behind us, I threw myself into Christmas preparations with the fervor of someone trying to outrun sadness. Christmas has always been my holiday. I loved everything about it—the lights twinkling in the December darkness, the evergreen garlands smelling of cedar, and tinsel on the tree echoing the holidays of my 1970s childhood. I took a lot of joy creating the magic for my children.

In early December, I brought out the decorations. When David and I had divided our possessions, less than two months earlier, we decided to wait until the holidays to open this box. I had accumulated many ornaments from my childhood, which my mom passed on to me when I moved into my own place. I often brought back an ornament from special trips. Of course, all the handmade ornaments from the kids were the most-prized possession in the box. And so, the task of division begins again.

"Hey," I inquired over text (our least volatile communication tool at the time), "I just took out the Christmas decorations and want to be sure you have what you need to make Christmas happen over at your place. Would you like to get together and go through the box?"

It was a sincere invitation, and a totally inappropriate, controlling nudge to ensure that he would make Christmas "happen" at his house. These were the early days, so it felt totally natural to be slightly distracted, and at times consumed, wondering what was happening at the other house. This was a big holiday for the kids, and I usually took the lead, would he get it "right"?

I reminded myself, his home is not my responsibility, nor should it be my worry. It was easier said than done.

"Not necessary," came his reply. "You can just put together a box of stuff, and I will pick it up the next time I grab the kids." Probably for the best. The separation was like a wound that hadn't yet healed. So, picking at the scab of divorce pain was likely going to lead to more pain. It takes such immense restraint not to pick at the scab. I was seldom successful in those early months.

I did as he requested and put together a thoughtfully curated box with a mix of lights, garland, and ornaments. He had a few sentimental ornaments from his former life mingled in, and I extracted those as well. I added a new box of tinsel on top, another well-intentioned yet misplaced nudge.

When I brought out the box of decorations, the kids plunged in, pulling out familiar ornaments and exclaiming over each discovery. "Look, Mom, the reindeer I made!" Dwyer held up a popsicle stick creation from preschool, liberally coated in glitter and missing one googly eye. Those precious creations had the fingerprints of their childhood baked into them.

"And here are my fancy snowflakes from last year!" Anya added, holding up the delicate creation she'd made in first grade.

This year brought new additions—Anya had crafted a felt Christmas tree in her second-grade class, decorated with glued-on sequins. Dwyer contributed a green handprint on hot-pink paper, edged in green glitter, with a red ribbon glued to the middle. Any parent will tell you that these are the masterpieces of your family collection. How would we "divide" the future works of art created by our kids?

I put a classic Christmas CD into the stereo, and "White Christmas" came crooning into the living room like a warm winter blanket. We were doing it. I was doing it. I was making Christmas happen here, in my home, in my way. That's what I could control.

We worked our way through the boxes methodically. Dwyer insisted on hanging all the candy canes at his eye level, creating a band of red and white around the lower third of the tree. Anya took charge of the delicate ornaments, carefully placing glass icicles and ceramic angels on the higher branches.

"Oh Anya, don't forget your new one," I said, noticing she hadn't hung it on the tree yet. She walked over to me, and I handed it to her.

She shuffled back to the tree and after a moment of quiet debate, she placed it carefully front and center. Then her shoulders slumped. She went and sat down on the sofa. I noticed tears in her eyes.

"Daddo's not here. It's not real Christmas, without him," she said, her voice breaking.

Her words took the wind out of me. I felt like I'd been stabbed in the chest. I went to her on the couch, wrapping an arm around her. Dwyer stopped and curled up under my other arm.

"Daddo will be here, Christmas morning," I tried to reassure her. "He'll be here to see the tree all finished and beautiful. We'll all be together then."

"But not now," Anya said, leaning into me.

"Nope, not now," I admitted.

"But you will get to decorate with Daddo and make that space really special with him." I could see and feel her pain. I wanted to lift it off her shoulders. Make it all better. It took time for the tears to subside, for the acute grief to soften back into the background ache we were all learning to live with. Eventually, we returned to decorating, though the earlier joy felt muted. When we finally finished, we stepped back to get a look at our handiwork.

"Do you think Santa will like it?" I asked, wondering how they were both feeling.

"It's pretty," Anya said, her voice steadier than earlier.

"Super fancy!" Dwyer added, already recovering with the resilience of a five-year-old kid.

We stood there together, my arms around both of them, looking at our tree.

Later that night, I lay in my bed and let the tears come. Anya's words about David not being there with us, repeating in my mind like a scratched record. I was grieving the ease and joy of the past Christmases we shared together. I was also grieving the Christmas moments that would never be.

CHRISTMAS MORNING

Once the kids woke up, they were instructed to come hop in bed with me, so we could call Daddo and tell him to come over. We would wait in the bedroom until he arrived, HO-HO-HO-ing his way through the front door.

"Merry Christmas, Mama!" Dwyer bounced onto the bed, his five-year-old energy impossible to contain.

"Merry Christmas!" I said, making room for both of them under the covers.

"Can we call Daddo now?" Anya asked, already reaching for the phone on my nightstand.

"Daddo! Daddo! Daddo!" Dwyer began chanting, bouncing with each syllable.

I dialed David's number, knowing he'd be waiting. He answered on the first ring. "Merry Christmas!" his voice boomed through the speaker.

"Come over! Come over!" both kids shouted.

"On my way!" he said. "Don't sneak into the living room without me!"

"We won't!" they promised, though I could see Dwyer already eyeing the door like he might make a break for the living room.

Eight minutes. That's how long it took David to drive from his home to mine, which felt like eight agonizing *days* for the kids. They stationed themselves at my bedroom window, noses pressed to the glass, breath fogging their view as they kept an eye on the driveway for Daddo's arrival. I put on sensible clothes (which is code for "a bra") in anticipation of spending the morning with my former husband. We were going to navigate the experiment of sharing this space and this day. Was there a protocol? Do I take his jacket and welcome him like a guest? Or does he just walk in like he always did? Once again, we were in new territory, trying to redefine boundaries around autonomous space that was recently shared space.

"He's here!" Anya shrieked, as David's car pulled into the driveway. They stood at my bedroom door, the threshold of a starting gate, waiting for the bell to ring, signaling the "All clear."

DING DONG! The door was unlocked, so he let himself in, as I hoped he would.

"Ho, ho, ho! Merry Christmas!" he said, scooping Anya up into his arms. Dwyer went straight to the tree and began investigating the new additions.

I followed behind and took in the scene. A family scene: two children showered with the love of their parents and excitement of Christmas, two parents standing together, apart. I struggled to digest the braid of pain and joy living inside my soul.

The kids took turns opening gifts, leaving the stockings for last, per family tradition. I flopped into the glider rocker, which had been a baby gift to our family when Anya was born. I spent many sleep-deprived nights nursing the babies in that chair. It was one of the things I wanted to keep in the house. I feel very attached to the stories this piece of furniture carries. It's likely I wouldn't have noticed the value and importance of that chair, until it became an *asset*. Fortunately, I was divorcing a sensible man, who whole-heartedly supported me keeping my baby-mama rocker.

David settled onto the big couch, the matching love seat now a fixture in his home. (Even the couches got divorced.) The kids were pinging between us, showing off their treasures. We watched our kids with shared delight. There were no remnants of divorce drama floating around the room. We were on stage. The day was about our kids, not us.

I won't lie; it wasn't easy. Those early months' post-separation, with the added stress of the holidays, were emotionally complex and very difficult to navigate so many conflicting emotions, on what was already a very emotional day.

But there we were, together yet apart. That was the goal. Could we keep our shit together enough to not destroy Christmas, and maybe even make it magical? David and I had coordinated everything via email—the big gifts from Santa, the smaller ones from us, a rundown on what we were doing independently, ensuring no duplication or disappointment. It simply wouldn't be cool if one of us gifted the kids an electric scooter and the other a box of bubbles.

Without prompting, the kids came running up to us with presents from them.

"Come sit next to Daddo," came Anya's in-charge voice, "That way we can give you your presents together," with extra emphasis on the word *together.*

After a quick recovery from the emotional slaying my six-year-old just gave me, I hoisted myself off the rocker and moved onto the couch next to David. If there is such a thing as an energy force field between people, we definitely had it between us. Despite the emotional turbulence we were feeling internally, we both played our onstage parenting role without fail. It allowed Christmas to be really joyful for our kids, without parental distraction.

"Mama, this is the one I made in Ms. Ella's class." Dwyer declared, with such pride and enthusiasm. "Daddo is going to get one just like it because Ms. Ella let me make two, one for each house. And Daddo already knows because he helped me wrap it up for you." Without pause, he continued on, "Daddo! Mama! Open them together."

We both did, and sighed, together.

We held back the tears, as we each held a bright green wreath made of little puzzle pieces randomly glued together on a small, round cardboard template and a big red bow smashed into the middle. This precious piece of art just became a family heirloom, and I was grateful I didn't have to divide this one.

Anya leapt into my vision holding a wrapped shoe box, "Mama this is for you from me. But not Dwyer." And she gave her little brother a sideways glance and a giggle.

"Thank you, Anya, that's so nice of you to go Christmas shopping for me," I commented, as I started to unwrap the Peanuts Christmas wrapping paper and raised an eyebrow of appreciation towards David.

"Daddo helped, he had to do the driving. Hurry up! You can rip it open, you know!" she exclaimed, her little body prancing around in rhythm with her words.

I opened the box and held up one fuzzy slipper, size nine. "This is perfect Anya, my favorite kind of slippers." Taking the bait, like all good mothers should, "Just one problem … I only have one slipper. That's not going to work out very well."

The kids were bursting with delight, so excited that they had concocted this hysterical prank for me on Christmas morning.

"Wait Mama, wait wait wait … now you can open my present," as Dwyer handed me a large, oversized box, he shot a look towards his big sister. Those two were bonded by mischief. Dwyer helped me tear into the snowman wrapping paper only to reveal another box inside the big box. This time a shoe box. "You're really gonna like this Mama, soooo sooooo much."

We all squealed in delight when I lifted the lid to reveal the other matching slipper. I promptly put on my slippers and chased them up and down the hallway making fuzzy slipper sounds, arms waving in the air, and kids stumbling around drunk with laughter. From the couch, David was recording the whole scene.

GIFT GIVING

David and I have always worked together to make memories for our kids, which is still part of our co-parent job-description. We intentionally and thoughtfully crafted gift-giving for our children, so they would feel successful. Also, part of our parental job description, whether married or not.

It went something like this (via text):

K: Hey, thanks for talking through presents for the kids, that was help-ful. I will happily grab all the stocking stuffers. Speaking of presents, the kids are going to want to give us gifts, and I think we should help make that happen. What do you think?

D: What did you have in mind?

K: Pretty much the same as before. I will take the kids shopping for you and help them wrap everything up and put it under the tree. We will probably also make something for you, and they will likely bring home some crafty stuff from school that can be gifted. The only difference is that now we pick our own gift and pay for our own gift. Just tell me what you want and where to get it, you can reimburse me afterwards. Kids and I will "go shopping" for you and take it from there.

D: Works for me.

K: Great. I would like the fuzzy slippers from Costco, size 9. They are there now, for about $30, but they will go fast. If you can't get out there soon, let me know. I will swing by and grab them. I can just leave them in a bag on your front porch. LMK

D: Pretty sure I can get out there with the kids.

K: Oh, one more idea—it might be fun for them to split the gift, and each give me one slipper.

CHRISTMAS DAY

Dwyer and David started putting together the tabletop Foosball game. Anya was busy with her new American Girl Doll, complete with bunk beds. We both jockeyed for photos when the kids took a breath, but we tried not to be overbearing as we clamored to capture each rare and fleeting moment. Would we still share photos? Was that allowed in the divorce handbook?

We decided to write our own handbook, so, of course, we shared photos from that day, and all subsequent special moments to come.

At 10 a.m., the grandparents arrived, strategically invited after the flurry of wrapping paper had come to rest on the living room floor. They were going through their own version of navigating our divorce and the emotional transition from in-laws to out-laws. We wanted to have the morning for the four of us, as more people would've created a room with more distractions. We were figuring things out; we didn't need an audience.

By mid-morning, we were ready to change things up. The room filled with additional voices, additional warmth, and I felt some of the tension ease. All the grandparents were friendly and kind, as always. My dad was a water specialist and was known to say, "The solution to pollution is dilution." With others present, David and I would be on our best behavior, and there were other people to dilute any anger, sadness, or resentment between us. It worked.

The grandparents sat in the living room watching David and Dwyer continue to build the Foosball table. Anya was now giving a fashion show with her new doll. I delivered plates of scrambled eggs, fruit, and coffee cake to everyone. The kids plowed through the gifts from their grandparents and then plowed through their plates. They were deep into playing with new toys, all the presents had been opened, and everyone was stuffed from brunch. It was time to quit while we were ahead. I could tell David was antsy and ready to go. We decided it would be best if all the grandparents and David left together in one jolly holiday exit.

At the door before he left, I told him, "Thanks for making this work. It was a great day for the kids. I know it's hard to be the one to leave today." And I meant it. I was grateful we could have Christmas together, as one family, and I was grateful I wasn't the one leaving on our first Christmas in the new world.

"I agree, a good day," he replied, and I could see he meant it too. "Same plan next year?"

"Same plan."

CHRISTMAS YET TO COME

This pattern continued for the next six years. We alternated who hosted, but it was always the same morning routine: kids would crawl into bed, call the other parent, wait for their arrival, all open presents together, and then share a meal with the grandparents. A couple of years down the road, we dropped the grandparents as an essential ingredient. As the years progressed, we required less dilution in our little family pond.

The stocking stuffers became my domain entirely. We'd set a budget—$50 per child—and I'd shop for both houses, delivering a bag of wrapped trinkets to David's door each December 23rd. At first, this felt like another example of household labor falling to me. Why was I still the one making Christmas magic happen? Why couldn't he remember to buy stocking stuffers for his own house? The old tune of resentment was becoming the soundtrack in my head.

But somewhere around year three, I had an epiphany. I loved Christmas shopping. I loved finding the perfect silly socks, the tiny puzzles, the chocolate coins. I was good at it, and I enjoyed it. Why was I hanging on to this resentment? David had never been highly engaged with Christmas preparations. Why would I think that would change now? Even *if* I had fully relinquished the Christmas planning power, I would still be directing from the wings and disappointed that he didn't do more. It's also one of his busiest times of year at work. So, I took the lead without resentment and committed to be in the delight of making Christmas happen for our family. Not in spite of David, but in support of him.

David and I swapped who hosted Christmas in Missoula until 2017, when Anya and Dwyer were 12 and 11, respectively. The cat was out of the bag on Santa by then—"keeping the magic of Christmas alive" is harder with tweens. One night after a school event in October, the kids approached David and me with a proposal. We were discussing holiday plans, and Anya, ever the diplomat, spoke up.

"We've been talking," she began, looking to Dwyer for support. "And we have an idea for the holidays."

"Oh," I said carefully. "What's your idea?" I glanced at David who had raised an eyebrow.

"Well, Thanksgiving with Dad's family is always really cool and awesome with all the food, and the music, and the cousins, and the slumber party, ya know, it's great." Dwyer hesitated cautiously, wondering if he had gushed too much, sensitive to my feelings. It's a burden that children of divorce seem to carry, regardless of our efforts to try and release them from this responsibility.

"Oh yeah, I get it," agreeing with him. "Dad's family hosts a great Thanksgiving. My family, on the other hand, is kind of a dud."

"Yeah, we kinda agree," by which she meant, we totally agree. "We were wondering if we could do Christmas with you and Thanksgiving with Dad." The words tumbled out quickly, like she was afraid she'd lose courage if she paused. "It's just—Thanksgiving with the cousins is so fun, and Christmas at Mamma's is special in a different way. This way, we don't have to alternate, and everyone knows what to expect."

I looked at David, who seemed as surprised as I was. Our children had found their own solution and their own voice. We said we would talk about it and get back to them. Handling it this way helps avoid the unfortunate moment when you realize you aren't in alignment about something, and the kids having to watch the debate play out in front of them. Save those moments for offstage.

And so, our holiday pattern evolved. Thanksgiving became David's domain entirely, and Christmas became mine. David would still pop in on Christmas morning and often spend just a couple hours with us and then leave to work extra holiday shifts, relieving his staff who desperately wanted the time off.

Eventually, I asked David how he felt about me leaving with the kids over the Christmas break. Without hesitation, he agreed, probably relieved to move on from his least favorite holiday. Our first trip was to visit my sister and brother in NYC. The kids and I went to see *Harry Potter* on Broadway and the *Rockefeller Christmas Spectacular.* The next year, we went to San Francisco to see my other brother's family and had the chance to see the national tour of *Hamilton* and a *Cirque du Soleil* show. Those were great memory-making trips, and I never felt a hint of resentment from David, only outward support and enthusiasm.

We had found a new way through the holidays. Our way.

AUTHOR BIO

Karen McNenny is the founder of The Good Divorce Academy and host of *The Good Divorce Show*, where she brings warmth, honesty, and practical insight to modern co-parenting. As a mediator and divorce consultant, she helps families navigate separation with more steadiness, respect, and compassion. She is a social activist working towards world peace, one relationship at a time. You can find Karen running with scissors through the Rocky Mountain West.

INDEX